MW00979828

THE WORDS YOU CONFUSE

ELYSE SOMMER

BOB ADAMS, INC.
PUBLISHERS
Holbrook, Massachusetts

Copyright ©1992, Elyse Sommer. All rights reserved. No part of this work may be reproduced in any form, or by any means, without the permission of the publisher. Exceptions are made for brief excerpts to be used in published reviews.

Published by Bob Adams, Inc.
260 Center Street, Holbrook, MA 02343

ISBN: 1-55850-158-4

Printed in the United States of America

A B C D E F G H I J

Contents

A word is not a crystal, transparent and unchanged, it is the skin of a living thought and may vary greatly in color and content according to the circumstances and the time in which it is used.

—*Justice Oliver Wendell Holmes*

The difference between the right word and the almost right word is the difference between lightning and the lightning bug.

— *Mark Twain*

Introduction

When enough people confuse one word or expression with another, misuse sometimes metamorphoses into common usage. That's not to say that distinctions in meaning no longer matter. On the contrary, precise word use is a top-ranking criterion for evaluating ability and intelligence in school, the workplace or social situations. This book attempts to take the confusion out of some of the most frequently misused and confused words encountered in everyday modern life. I do not offer a substitute for a dictionary with its exhaustive definitions of every meaning of every word in the language, but a complement. Think of it, if you will, as an abridged "precisionary" of the most typical and common problem word groups defined to elucidate the riddle of the precisely right word choice.

Unlike a dictionary, which lists all words in strict alphabetical order, these entries are organized into word groups so that their similarities and distinctions are instantly apparent. You won't need to browse far through this main section to realize that much misuse and confusion has its root cause in one of the following: words that look alike, words that sound alike, words with meanings separated by a very fine line of distinction, precise meanings entombed in foreignisms and acronyms, and vague uncertainties pertaining to grammatical correctness.

To increase your enjoyment of this book I've cooked up a dessert to top off the main entries. While this concoction, which I call the Rhymed Review, would hardly rate five stars in a Michelin guide of prosody, it will nourish your powers of precision. And so, *bon appétit* . . . or, to be more precise, *bon mot.*

Elyse Sommer
Forest Hills, New York ● Lee, Massachusetts

THE WORDS
YOU CONFUSE

A User's Guide to Organization and Use

How to Find a Word

All entries are organized into word groups and alphabetized according to the first word in that group; for example, *synopsis* is grouped with *abridgment*. The index at the end of the book lists every defined word in alphabetical order. If the word is the second or third in a group, the first word, under which the group is alphabetized, is listed next to it in parenthesis. Thus the index lists *abridgment* by itself and *synopsis* as *synopsis (abridgment)*.

About the Entry Format

- ☐ Each word is followed by a concise definition and in most instances an illustrative phrase or sentence flagged by the symbol: ✎.

- ☐ Illustrative sentences that feature more than one defined word follow the last word's definition and are preceded by one ✎ symbol for each word illustrated.

- ☐ Any additional information is preceded by the symbol ✪.

For details about the rhymed review format, see the introductory text of that section.

abdicate To formally renounce a high office or responsibility. ✎ He ABDICATED his presidency of the firm.

abrogate To do away with. ✎ The new president ABROGATED the old hiring system.

arrogate To appropriate or claim unfairly. ✎ The president's appointees quickly ARROGATED the best offices to themselves.

abridgment Text that's been shortened. ✎ The ABRIDGMENT contained fifty pages less than the original.

excerpt A reproduction of part of a book, play, speech, or other work. ✎ The magazine EXCERPTED the novel's first chapter.

synopsis A summary of what a work is about. ✎ He submitted a SYNOPSIS and a sample chapter.

abyss A bottomless hole. ✎ She was in an ABYSS of grief.

vortex A whirlpool or whirlwind. ✎ They were sucked into a VORTEX of corruption.

ac Abbreviation for alternating current, which reverses itself periodically. It is used almost universally, with varying frequencies and voltages, for household and industrial power.

dc Abbreviation for direct current, which goes in one direction only, and usually comes from batteries.
✪ Modern slang usage has made ac/dc synonymous with "having dual sexual preferences."

acclimation The adjustment to a climate or situation. ✎ Her ACCLIMATION to country life happened in slow motion.

acculturation Process of adopting the social customs of a new culture or surroundings. ✎ The parents' ACCUL-

3

TURATION moved at a much slower pace than the children's.

accusation An allegation or charge of wrongdoing.
recrimination An accusation made in answer to another, a rebuttal.
✎ ✎ He met their ACCUSATION with RECRIMINATIONS about discriminatory practices.

acme The highest point or summit.
epitome The embodiment or consummate representation of something; popular in its verb form, to epitomize.
✎ ✎ He EPITOMIZED the sort of person who would stop at nothing to reach the ACME of his ambitions.
○ See also *nadir*.

acquiescent Behaving compliantly. ✎ He found the students ACQUIESCENT but somewhat dull.
quiescent Temporarily at rest. ✎ His disease, though chronic, had been QUIESCENT for some time.

acronym A word or abbreviation formed by blending the first letters of several words. The trick is to come up with a meaningful new word which, like the second example below, no longer requires an initial capital: ✎ NOW (National Organization for Women); ✎ LASER (light amplification by stimulation of emission radiation).
portmanteau word Not a fancy substitute for an acronym but a word formed by blending parts of two words into a new one. ✎ BRUNCH (breakfast and lunch); ✎ CHORTLE (chuckle and snort).

across-the-board A horse-racing bet on one horse to come in first (win), second (place), or third (show); also used generally for anything all-inclusive. ✎ Salary cuts went ACROSS-THE-BOARD, from mailroom to boardroom.
on the nose A horse-racing bet on the first-place winner;

also used generally for perfectly correct or on time. ✎ His gut feelings about her proved to be right ON THE NOSE.

acute A sickness or flaw severe enough to require immediate action or intense reaction. ✎ With the closing of another plant, the town's fiscal problems became ACUTE.

chronic A long-term ailment or persistent failing. ✎ How can I believe a statement made by a CHRONIC liar?

ad hoc Involving a specific situation, and therefore more temporary than long-term. ✎ He appointed an AD HOC committee to look into the problem.

ad lib An unrehearsed remark. ✎ Don't expect to AD LIB your way through this meeting. We want facts!

adapt To modify or make fitting.

adept Highly competent.

✎✎ She was ADEPT at ADAPTING to new situations.

addict Someone compulsive. ✎ He is a gambling ADDICT.

devotee Someone passionately devoted to something or someone. ✎ Mary and Jim are theater DEVOTEES.

adduce To cite as a point of proof in an argument. ✎ We ADDUCED several reasons for his panic and earned him a reprieve from his boss.

deduce To reach a conclusion through reason. ✎ After careful observation, we DEDUCED it was all a scam.

adverse Unfavorably disposed. ✎ His proposal met with an extremely ADVERSE reaction.

averse Showing unwillingness or reluctance. ✎ I'm AVERSE to anything that will lead to violence.

aesthetic Relating to beauty and the appreciation thereof; also spelled esthetic. ✎ Though the show's tunes are just so-so, the set is an AESTHETIC treat.

5

ascetic Self-denying, comfort-rejecting behavior. ✎ There was nothing ASCETIC about his luxurious apartment.

affect To influence; also to assume, as a pose. ✎ On election day millions of voters AFFECT public policy. ✎ He AFFECTED a nonchalant manner.

effect To result in change. ✎ She EFFECTED many dramatic reforms. ✎ The EFFECT on us was dramatic.
○ Effect can be both noun and verb. Affect is always a verb in common usage, though it is used as a noun for emotion in the specialized language of psychology.

afflict To hurt physically or mentally. ✎ He was AFFLICTED with chronic back pain and bouts of depression.

inflict To impose an unwelcome burden or blow. ✎ The judge INFLICTED a stiff sentence.

aggravate To make worse; to exacerbate. ✎ Scratching a mosquito bite will only AGGRAVATE the itch.

irritate To annoy. ✎ Your constant nagging does more to IRRITATE than persuade me.

agnostic One who is convinced neither of the existence nor of the nonexistence of God.

atheist One who unconditionally denies the existence of God.
✎ ✎ Harry does not reject the idea of a higher diety. However, as an AGNOSTIC he feels certain only about material things. His friend Harry, an ATHIEST, firmly rejects any possibility of God's existence.

AIDS Acronym for Acquired Immune Deficiency Syndrome, the disease.

HIV Acronym for Human Immunodeficiency Virus, which causes AIDS.
✎ ✎ The fact that AIDS can strike anyone, was dramatically brought home to the public when Magic Johnson retired from basketball stardom after testing HIV-positive.

à la carte Restaurant term for a menu featuring individually priced dishes.

prix fixe Restaurant term for a fixed price, full course dinner.

✎ ✎ If we get to the restaurant before six, we can order the PRIX FIX special, which includes soup, salad, a main course, and dessert for $14.95. After six the menu is À LA CARTE, and the same meal will cost almost twice as much.

alibi A claim of innocence based on the accused's having been somewhere other than the scene of the crime. ✎ His ALIBI was as unshakable as granite.

excuse The reason given for not doing something or being some place. ✎ There's absolutely no EXCUSE for being late.

alien Someone living in a foreign country without citizenship. ✎ The prison systems in some states house many illegal ALIENS.

foreigner What we all are or may feel like when not in our native countries or a familiar setting. ✎ Disneyland is one of the chief attractions for FOREIGNERS who visit the United States.

✪ As adjectives, both *alien* and *foreigner* mean strange and different, but alien has the added association of something inconsistent or repugnant.

alliteration Term for repetition of the same consonant sound at the beginning of two or more words. ✎ Nattering nabobs of negativism.

assonance Repetition of vowel sounds. ✎ *so* and *though*. ✎ *roam* and *rove*.

✪ See also, *homograph*.

allusion An indirect but pointed reference; also a brief reference to a well-known or historic place, event or person. ✎ a Mona Lisa smile; ✎ She made an ALLUSION to

7

his mistake.

delusion A false, unrealistic, and persistent belief. ✎ He suffers from DELUSIONS of grandeur.

illusion A false or misleading impression. ✎ She creates the ILLUSION of youthfulness.

altercation A noisy, heated quarrel, more likely to be physical than a dispute. ✎ The teacher ended their AL-TERCATION.

dispute A disagreement or quarrel involving thought, such as a debate. ✎ We DISPUTED the merits of the case into the wee hours.

alternate By turns, one after the other. ✎ We visit them on ALTERNATE weekends.

alternative A choice between two situations. ✎ We had two ALTERNATIVES: flee or fight.

alto The lowest singing range for female singers.

contralto The deep, mellow, second-lowest female voice.

mezzo-soprano The sound range just below a soprano.

soprano The highest female singing voice.

> ✪ ALTO also refers to the musical instrument with the second highest pitch in its group, as *alto saxophone*.
> ✪ See also *baritone*.

all together All in a group in one place. ✎ It often takes a funeral to bring the family ALL TOGETHER.

altogether Completely; all told. ✎ I'm not ALTOGETHER certain that this is such a good idea.

alumna A female graduate.

alumnae More than one female graduate.

alumni More than one graduate at least one of whom is male.

alumnus A male graduate.

> ✎ ✎ ✎ ✎ Betty Brownell became an ALUMNA of a local junior college a year after her brother Tod became

an ALUMNUS. Betty and Tod's two older sisters are also ALUMNAE. All four Brownells went on to become ALUMNI of the state university.

amateur A nonprofessional participant in an activity. ✎ He played as well and as regularly as a pro, but maintained his AMATEUR standing.

novice A beginner in any field of endeavor who may become an expert with professional or amateur status. ✎ Even with his immense gifts firmly established, he felt as vulnerable to failure as a NOVICE.

ambiguous Unclear in meaning or behavior. ✎ Your letter was so AMBIGUOUS that I'm still not sure what you meant.

ambivalent Having unclear or mixed feelings. ✎ I love him but I'm AMBIVALENT about marrying him.

ambrosia A word used by the ancient Greeks for food fit for the gods, currently applied to any food that tastes and smells exceptionally good. ✎ He is a talented cook who can impart the aroma and taste of the finest AMBROSIA to a very simple meal.

nectar A liquid counterpart of ambrosia, with the added meaning of being invigorating or healthful—probably because nectars are usually made from fruit juices. ✎ She concoted a sparkling NECTAR of freshly squeezed fruit poured over finely crushed ice.

American Plan Hotel accommodations that provide room, service, and all meals for a fixed price.

European Plan Hotels offering this plan may have one or more restaurants, but meals there are not covered by the room rates. Some such hotels do offer a "bed and breakfast" rate.

Modified American Plan American Plan accommodations, but without a midday meal.

amicable Interacting in an agreeable, amiable manner.
inimical This means the very opposite of agreeable; un-
friendly.
   ✎ ✎ Our AMICABLE first meeting did not prepare me
for his INIMICAL attitude when we met again.

ammunition The materials fired from fighting weapons;
also any other means of defense, from stones to verbal
weapons. ✎ Education is the best AMMUNITION against
poverty. ✎ Wit was his AMMUNITION.
munitions A more sweeping military term since it covers
both ammunition and weapons, but with little everyday
application. ✎ The smugglers had built up an arsenal of
MUNITIONS that included hand guns, rifles, and explo-
sives.

among Involving three or more people or objects. ✎ The
winnings were shared AMONG the six people who had
purchased the lottery ticket.
between Involving two people or objects, or sometimes
more than two if each pair is considered separately. ✎
This is strictly BETWEEN you and me! ✎ The treaty pro-
motes cultural exchanges BETWEEN the three countries.

amount How much (weighed or measured)?
number How many (counted)?
   ✎ ✎ For such a small NUMBER of applicants, they
used up a large AMOUNT of our interviewing budget.

amps Abbreviation for amperes, the measure of electrical
current.
ohms These measure the resistance that slows the flow of
current.
volts The measurement of the pressure that moves the current through the circuit.
watts The amount of power an electrical device uses—at
the same voltage. ✎ A computer with a 150-WATT
power supply uses more current than one with a 120-

WATT supply.

✎ ✎ ✎ ✎ Each AMP that flows along the wires of your house represents a unit of electric current, and each OHM is a unit of resistance. If AMPS were water, VOLTS would be the water pressure forcing the current through the pipes of your house. Your electricity bill is determined by the amount of energy required to produce 1,000 WATTS of power.

analogous Similar enough to permit one to draw a fitting comparison. ✎ To say sexual harassment in the workplace does not exist is ANALOGOUS to saying women don't work for money.

parallel Exactly alike in direction or inclination. ✎ Their careers moved along parallel paths.

anathema Any object of intense dislike, human or otherwise.

plethora Too much, even if it's a good thing.

✎ ✎ A PLETHORA of luxuries was ANATHEMA to her new, simplified lifestyle.

anchor A heavy object that keeps a vessel from drifting; generally speaking, any source of stability. ✎ He was my only ANCHOR in a sea of despair and trouble.

buoy A device used as a ship's navigational marker or to keep a person afloat; generally speaking, a source of cheer and uplift. ✎ His visits never failed to BUOY my spirits.

android A robot built to look and act like a human.

automaton A robot-like machine that doesn't need to be plugged in or programmed to work; also used figuratively. ✎ To move around like an AUTOMATON.

anemometer Measures the speed of the wind.

barometer Measures air pressure.

ceilometer Measures cloud height.

hygrometer Measures humidity.

pluviometer Measures rainfall.
voltmeter Measures the electrical potential of volts.

◉ A barometer is the only one of these meteorological tools commonly found in a home.

annual Occurring once a year. ✏ an ANNUAL visit; ✏ an ANNUAL plant that blooms for a single season.
perennial Continuing throughout the year or longer. ✏ PERENNIALS that rebloom each year; ✏ a PERENNIAL source of pleasure.

antibody A special protein produced by the body's immune system that fight foreign substances.
antigen A foreign substance that stimulates antibodies.

✏ ✏ He was treated with ANTIGENS to restore ANTI-BODIES to his impaired immune system.

antiques Legally, objects at least one hundred years old; to the connoisseur, finely crafted objects made before 1830. ✏ The dealer purchased the entire contents of the house in order to obtain two valuable eighteenth century AN-TIQUE chairs.
collectibles A catchall term for everything with any historical or investment interest. ✏ Their home was filled with interesting COLLECTIBLES. Though most items were no more than twenty years old, some had already increased in value since they were bought at various flea markets.
heirlooms Objects younger than antiques, older than collectibles, with the value often determined by sentiment or fine workmanship. ✏ Although the quilt made by my grandmother is somewhat tattered, it is one of my most treasured HEIRLOOMS.

anxious Uneasy. ✏ to have an ANXIOUS moment.
eager To be enthusiastic. ✏ to be EAGER to please.

◉ Usage has given *anxious* the secondary meaning of

12

being a synonym of eager. However, to be absolutely precise, pair eager only with enthusiasm. ✎ ✎ She was EAGER to marry him, but ANXIOUS about her mother's disapproval.

apogee Astronomically, the point when an orbiting body, like the moon or a planet, is furthest from the earth, and thus the peak of anything.
perigee The opposite of apogee; the lowest point of anything.
   ✎ ✎ In just one year he tumbled from the APOGEE of power to the PERIGEE.

apostate One who abandons a basic belief or principle.
   ✎ He was condemned as an APOSTATE from liberalism.
apostle When not capitalized to identify one of the twelve men chosen by Christ to preach His gospel, this refers to someone who leads a new and usually moral cause. ✎ He was an APOSTLE of vegetarianism.

apple cider Unpasteurized apple juice that becomes hard cider once it ages and ferments and cider vinegar when it's fully fermented.
apple juice Apples that are ground up and pressed to extract the juice, which is pasteurized and hermetically sealed in a bottle or can.

apposite Well-placed or suitable.
opposite Contrary or different.
   ✎ ✎ They shared APPOSITE goals, but had OPPOSITE strategies for attaining them.
   ✪ To keep the distinction clear, think of AA for apposite and apt, and OO for opposite and other.

appraise To evaluate.
apprise To inform or give notice.

✎ ✎ I asked him to APPRAISE my methods and AP-PRISE me of whether I was on the right track.

arbitrator An impartial judge chosen by the parties of a dispute to make a decision by which they agree to be bound. Arbitrator, or arbiter, can also be used to refer to anyone considered an influential authority: ✎ an ARBITER of taste.

mediator Like an arbitrator, but more active in making proposals and without binding authority.

✎ ✎ Lacking an ARBITER's power to make a decision, the MEDIATOR failed to have his excellent suggestions implemented.

arcane Mysterious. ✎ The group's ARCANE rituals are known only to its members.

archaic Out of date. ✎ Computers have made manual typewriters ARCHAIC.

articulate Fluent and clear.

eloquent Forcefully convincing.

✎ ✎ A manual writer must be ARTICULATE; a speech writer should also be ELOQUENT.

as far as Use this to express distance.

so far as Use this to express degree or extent.

✎ ✎ SO FAR AS we know nothing would be gained from going further; therefore, this is AS FAR AS we're going to take it.

ascertain To find out definitely, to make certain.

inquire To ask questions for a variety of reasons, which could include wanting to ascertain facts.

✎ ✎ After she ASCERTAINED that he was ill, she IN-QUIRED whether she could do something to help.

assemblage A sculptural artwork created by grouping together unrelated objects. ✎ His ASSEMBLAGES contained weathered wood, driftwood, stones, and other materials found along the shore.

collage An artwork created by mounting related materials on a backing. ✎ Cut and torn papers are key materials used by those who work in COLLAGE.

decoupage Applying paper cutouts to a surface and embedding them in varnish to simulate a painted finish. ✎ Venetian furniture craftsmen, unable to create the elaborately painted surfaces popular during the eighteenth century, invented DECOUPAGE. Their cut-and-paste "painting" then developed into a hobby for French and English ladies of leisure.

✪ Both collage and assemblage are used as everyday words for any collection, as of facts or methods. ✎ ✎ The conference brought together an ASSEMBLAGE of differing views to deal with a COLLAGE of options.

assure To make certain or to state with confidence. ✎ He ASSURED them that their investment was safe.

insure Stronger than assure because it's usually accompanied by a written contract. ✎ It's best to INSURE all your valuables.

asteroid The larger fragments of the rocky debris of the solar system that never quite became planets.

meteor A fiery glow (caused by a meteoroid) that passes through the earth's atmosphere. It is popularly known as a shooting star.

meteorite A meteoroid that plunges to earth as a metal or rock.

meteoroid Any small celestial object from a tiny particle to an asteroid, that causes a meteor.

✎ ✎ ✎ ✎ The thousands of ASTEROIDS in orbit range from 1,000 kilometers to less than 1 kilometer in diameter. Loosely speaking, the word METEOR is often also used to apply to METEROIDS and METEORITES.

astonished Surprised.
astounded Extremely surprised.
dumfounded Stunned if not speechless from surprise; also
    spelled *dumbfounded*.
       ✎ ✎ ✎ We were ASTONISHED by her progress, AS-
    TOUNDED at her talent, and DUMFOUNDED by her disap-
    pearance from the performing arts scene.

astrology Attempts to foretell the future or judge people's
    character by the stars.
astronomy The scientific study of the planets, stars, and
    other celestial bodies and phenomena.

atlas A book of maps and related illustrative matter.
gazetteer A dictionary of geographical names and data.
     ✪ See also, *dictionary*.

attribute To assign a cause or origin to something or some-
    one. ✎ The remark was ATTRIBUTED to a source close
    to the president.
impute To assign or attribute, with negative implication. ✎
    Why do you IMPUTE insincere motives to me?
     ✪ See also *imply*.

aurora australis A broad display of rather faint light in
    the southern hemisphere at night.
aurora borealis Like the above but in the northern
    hemipshere; also called Northern Lights.

authentic Exactly as represented, genuine. ✎ Is that an
    AUTHENTIC Picasso?
authoritarian Dominating in manner. ✎ They did not ap-
    preciate his AUTHORITARIAN methods.
authoritative Having enough substance to command respect.
     ✎ He quoted from several AUTHORITATIVE sources.

avert To prevent or turn away. ✎ You can't evade a prob-
    lem simply by AVERTING your eyes from it.

16

avoid To bypass. He AVOIDED trouble by walking only down well-lit streets.

B

backlist Books not dependent on timeliness and thus apt to exist beyond the season when they're published. The Bible and standard reference works such as dictionaries are strong BACKLIST sellers.

frontlist Books published during the current season, which may or may not remain in print as backlist titles. Best-selling novels or books published to tie in with a fad typify FRONTLIST books.

badger To harass someone to obtain a desired response.

bait To tempt or torment to obtain a desired result.
     Her boss BADGERED her for dates. He tried to BAIT her first with promises of promotion, later with unpleasant remarks.

bagel A doughnut-shaped roll boiled in water and baked; currently available in many varieties—whole wheat, pumpernickel, raisin, etc.

bialy A baked roll with a depression in its center, either plain or onion flavored; unlike the bagel, available mainly in Jewish neighborhoods.

baleful Destructive or threatening; baneful. His BALEFUL expression frightened the children.

doleful Expression of grief or great sadness. Her DOLEFUL brown eyes reflected years of suffering.

baluster A support post.

balustrade The support posts and rail for a balcony or terrace.

banister The supports for a staircase handrail often used to refer to the support posts and the rail.
○ *Bannister*, acceptable alternative spelling.

baritone The second-lowest range, deeper than a tenor but higher than a bass.
bass The lowest range of a man's voice.
falsetto An artificially high voice developed by tenors who want to exceed their highest natural range.
tenor The highest-ranging common male voice.

bathos Excessive sentimentality or triviality. ✎ The movie practically drowned its characters in BATHOS.
pathos Feeling of compassion or concern. ✎ They felt great PATHOS for the refugees.

bears Speculators who sell stocks expecting to buy them back at even lower prices, a plan based on a gloomy or "bearish" economic view.
bulls Optimistic or "bullish" speculators who buy stocks with the expectation of rising prices.
○ Both terms, especially the second, are often used as adjectives to express a generally optimistic or pessimistic economic viewpoint. ✎ A flurry of home sales made many economists feel more BULLISH than they had in a while.

befuddled In a state of confusion. ✎ I was completely BEFUDDLED by the sudden turn of events.
bemused Lost in thought; also bewildered. ✎ He seemed too BEMUSED to notice our distress.

bellwether A symbol of leadership, from its original meaning for a flock's leading sheep.
harbinger Something or someone signaling change.
✎ ✎ If large companies are to be regarded as BELLWETHERS of the economy in general, the wave of firings may be regarded as a HARBINGER of wider unemployment.

○ Precisionists reserve bellwether for the messenger of change and harbinger for the alarm bell.

beltway An expressway circling an urban area.
expressway Any multilane highway that expedites traffic.
freeway An expressway without tolls.

○ The beltway that takes people living in communities surrounding the nation's capital to and from work is so famous that it is often used figuratively to refer to government insiders. ✎ The rumor inside the BELTWAY is that the scandal will lead to a wave of Congressional resignations.

benchmark A surveyor's term for a marker that's widely used to express any hoped-for quality or objective. ✎ The restaurant's service may be taken as a BENCHMARK for its overall excellence.

hallmark A mark stamped on gold and silver articles that certifies quality or genuineness; also used more broadly to describe human characteristics. ✎ Trustworthiness is the HALLMARK of a good friend.

beside Use this when you mean at the side of. ✎ The bride stood BESIDE the groom.

besides Use this when you mean in addition to. ✎ She knew few people BESIDES her neighbors.

biannual Occurring twice a year. ✎ The author's contract calls for BIANNUAL royalty reports, one in March and one in December.

biennial Occurring every second year. ✎ She won first prize in the BIENNIAL small art work exhibition three times in a row—in 1986, 1988, and 1990.

semiannual Same as biannual. ✎ The shareholders met SEMIANNUALLY, in January and June.

○ Specify the exact period covered for all words beginning with BI or SEMI, as in the above examples. For a subscribers to a bimonthly magazine, for example, spell out whether they can expect an issue twice a month or once every second month; if a meeting is semiannual, the dates avoid ambiguity as to whether that means twice a year with one meeting every half year or twice during the middle of the year.

bit   Abbreviation for a single binary digit, the 0 or 1 character of a digital computer's notation system—the smallest.

byte   A group of bits—usually eight.

blizzard   A heavy and often damaging wind-driven snowstorm.

snowstorm   A snowfall without damaging winds.

✎ ✎ SNOWSTORMS are followed by kids on sleds; BLIZZARDS, by rescue teams.

blues   African-American type of rural southern folk song popularized early in this century. ✎ The "Memphis Blues" and the "St. Louis Blues" popularized the BLUES throughout the United States and earned their composer, W.C. Handy, the title "Father of the Blues."

rhythm & blues   A jazzy, danceable version of the blues; commonly known as R&B. ✎ R & B was developed by Count Basie in the 1930s.

❂ See also *pop*.

blush   To turn red from shame, embarrassment, or confusion. ✎ She BLUSHED when she realized her mistake.

flush   Like a blush, with the addition of excitement, anger, or fever as a cause. ✎ He was FLUSHED with triumph.

boat   A vessel too small to navigate anything but shallow, sheltered waters.

ship   A vessel large enough to navigate in deep water.

❂ In the Navy, a boat is generally identified as a vessel

that can be hauled aboard a ship. However, submarines are always referred to as boats.

boil To cook food in liquid that's kept at the bubbling point; more broadly, to show or express extreme anger. ✎ Her anger finally BOILED over.

simmer To cook food in liquid kept just below the boiling point; more broadly, to seethe with barely controlled anger. ✎ I SIMMERED with unspoken rage.

stew Food simmered in a covered dish for a long time; also informal expression for anxiety. ✎ I'm in a STEW about these endless delays.

boisterous Noisy, unrestrained behavior. ✎ The room was buzzing with their BOISTEROUS merrymaking.

obstreperous Like boisterous, but more aggressive and uncontrollable. ✎ The police had to restrain the OB-STREPEROUS gang on several occasions.

bombard To attack, though not necessarily with lethal weapons.

bombastic Adjective for a pompous speech or speaker. Do not substitute the nonexistent verb bombast!
✎ ✎ We were BOMBARDED with a barrage of boring and BOMBASTIC lectures.

book value What an entity's or individual's balance sheet shows as the total value, or the cost of all assets less the amount of depreciation.

market value What your assets would fetch if you sold them.
✎ ✎ The company's stock has a BOOK VALUE of $50 a share and a MARKET VALUE of $5.

booklet A small book with bound pages.

brochure A small unbound pamphlet.

boot, boot-up To turn on or load a computer's operating system.

21

cold boot To restart a computer after turning it off.

warm boot To turn the system off and on with keys on your keyboard instead of the on-off switch (usually by simultaneously pressing the CTRL-ALT-DEL keys).

✎ ✎ ✎ You usually BOOT UP with a COLD BOOT when you begin a day's work. If it becomes necessary to restart the system—for example, if your program freezes or misfunctions—it's best to try re-starting the system with a WARM BOOT which does not send a surge through the system as a COLD BOOT does.

born Pertaining to birth or natural ability: ✎ BORN during the night ✎ a BORN story teller.

borne Pertaining to something carried or endured: ✎ BORNE ashore ✎ too terrible to be BORNE.

bravado A boastful show of bravery. ✎ When the time came to act, his BRAVADO vanished like a wisp of vapor.

bravura A brilliant performance. ✎ The critics raved about the violinist's BRAVURA playing.

bring To produce or deliver something or someone readily available. ✎ Do BRING your friend along.

fetch To go get someone or something and bring it back. ✎ FETCH the ball, Fido!

brioche A small round roll or cake.

croissant A rich, crescent-shaped roll.

○ Both are French specialties. Croissants, the more popular, are currently available with fillings ranging from chocolate to broccoli.

broach To open up, as a discussion. ✎ As soon as she BROACHED the topic of marriage, he paled.

brooch A type of ornamental pin: ✎ a diamond BROOCH.

burn in A computer term for keeping a new system running long enough to make sure everything works; also the permanent imprinting of images onto your screen if you don't have a screen blanker. ✎ All reputable computer dealers will BURN IN a system before delivering it to a buyer.

burnout Condition suffered from job stress or overwork. ✎ One way to relieve BURNOUT caused by stressful assignments is to rotate people's job assignments; for example, putting a nurse working with terminally ill hospital patients on the maternity floor.

bush A very small shrub.
shrub A woody plant that's smaller than a tree.
shrubbery A collection of bushes and shrubs.

bushel Measurement of 4 pecks, 2150.42 cubic inches, or metrically, 35.238 liters.
peck Measurement of 8 quarts or 537.605 cubic inches, or its metric equivalent of 8.810 liters.
   ✪ To love someone a bushel and a peck, as in the famous show tune, means to love someone in a big way, (a bushel) and a small way (a peck).

butter Cooking ingredient and spread made by churning milk, cream, or a combination of both.
margarine Butter substitute made from vegetable, corn, or other oils, mixed with milk and salt.

butterfly A much-admired flying insect with large wings.
moth An unpopular butterfly lookalike that flies at night.

C

cache A hiding place or the things stashed away in it. ✎ They uncovered a CACHE of drugs.
cachet A mark or manner of distinction. ✎ To New York-

ers, a Park Avenue address has a CACHET of elegance.

cacophonous Dissonant, strident in sound. ✎ It was hard to hear each other over the CACOPHONOUS din.

euphonious Pleasantly melodic in sound. ✎ After the wedding guests were seated, a string quartet struck up the EUPHONIOUS notes of "I Love You Truly."

cadenza A musical solo in the midst of a performance to demonstrate a singer's or instrumentalist's skill.

glissando Another musical "show-off" term for rapid gliding movements, as on a piano; by extension, any rapid, smooth movements.

callous Hardened and unsympathetic, like a callous on one's foot. ✎ He was too CALLOUS to be moved by their plight.

callow Lacking in depth because of immaturity or inexperience. ✎ At sixteen, he was considered too CALLOW to be taken seriously.

calumny A false accusation or statement.
ignominy A disgrace.
　　✎ ✎ When their CALUMNY was finally exposed, she remained bitter about the years of IGNOMINY they had caused her.

canape A one- or two-bite appetizer made with bread, crackers, or pastry and eaten as a finger food.

hors d'oeuvres Catchall for any food served as an appetizer.
　　✎ ✎ The dinner party began with drinks and a tray of CANAPES that included a variety of spreads on crackers and breads. Later we had marinated mushrooms as HORS D'OEVRES followed by a wonderful veal roast and homemade ice cream.
　　❍ It's common to ask guests to come for "drinks and hors d'oeuvres" but no one says "come for canapes."

24

canvas Heavy coarse fabric: ✎ a CANVAS bag ✎ a painter's CANVAS.
canvass To solicit votes or information. ✎ to CANVASS a district for a polling organization.

canyon A very deep and narrow valley.
dell A small wooded valley.
glen A narrow valley.
gorge An extremely steep valley.

capital The city where a government conducts its business, a person's assets, or an adjective for a good idea. ✎ Albany is the CAPITAL of New York. ✎ It's a CAPITAL idea to invest your CAPITAL wisely.
capitol The building in which a legislature meets.
    ✎ The United States has many CAPITOLS, but CAPITOL, unlike CAPITAL, has only one meaning.

caplet A blended or portmanteau word coined by the makers of Tylenol for a capsule-shaped tablet.
capsule A case or covering for seeds or a dose of medicine.

cappuccino Espresso plus steaming hot milk with a touch of cinnamon and cocoa, served in a cup or mug.
espresso Coffee prepared in a machine using pressure to force steam over finely ground beans and served in small cups with a twist of lemon.

capricious Tending to sudden, surprising mood shifts.
malicious Tending to mean-spiritedness.
    ✎ ✎ His CAPRICIOUS behavior may not be MALICIOUS, but it's certainly disconcerting.

capstone The stone that tops off a structure; a person or group's highest achievement. ✎ The play is the CAPSTONE to date of an illustrious career.
keystone The stone at the top of an arch that holds it to-

25

gether; can also refer to a key principle. ✎ Health-care reform is the KEYSTONE of his campaign.

milestone An important event or turning point, though not necessarily the apex or capstone. ✎ The award marked a major MILESTONE in his career.

carat A gemstone measure. ✎ Her engagement ring was a three-CARAT, pear-shaped diamond.

caret A proofreader's mark to indicate an insertion. It looks like this: ^. ✎ The manuscript had little paper flags pasted near the CARETS in places where words had been omitted.

cardinal numbers The numbers that depict amounts: ✎ one, two, three.

ordinal numbers The numbers that depict position: ✎ first, second, third, fourth.

carnivorous Feeding on animal substances.
herbivorous Feeding on plants.
✎ ✎ Lions and tigers are CARNIVEROUS, as are cats and dogs. To the surprise of many, that mighty giant the elephant is HERBIVEROUS.

castigate To punish or criticize severely in order to correct. ✎ The senator was publicly CASTIGATED for taking advantage of his position.

denigrate To criticize in a demeaning, harmful manner. ✎ She DENIGRATED him in front of all his friends.

cave A natural hollow formed underground or in a hillside; in popular usage, to give in as the ground gives way to permit a cave to form: ✎ to CAVE in to someone's demands.

cavern A very large cave giving rise to the adjective *cavernous*, for any cavern-like chamber: ✎ CAVERNOUS halls.

caveat A warning. ✎ A few CAVEATS before you go.

caveat emptor A specific and well-known caveat, meaning "let the buyer beware!" ✎ Flea market shoppers should keep the motto *CAVEAT EMPTOR* in mind.

CD-ROM A compact disk (CD) used to store massive amounts of read-only memory (ROM) information. ✎ Consumers can now access encyclopedias, dictionaries and other large references on CD-ROM.

RAM Acronym for random access memory.

ROM Acronym for read-only memory, unchangeable machine-specific information.

　　✎ ✎ Programs built into a computer's ROM chips cannot be changed by the user. The programs used to create letters, spreadsheets, and other documents represent RAM information, which can be changed or stored as desired.

celestial Relating to the sky or heavens.

terrestrial Earthly, rather than heavenly.

　　✎ ✎ Steven Spielberg's famous E.T., the EXTRATERRESTRIAL, was a CELESTIAL visitor.

cement The binding agent that holds concrete together and thus anything that binds or holds together. ✎ Our relationship is CEMENTED by mutual respect.

concrete What you get when you mix gravel, sand, and cement; thus anything rock-hard or very solid: ✎ a CONCRETE driveway.

　　✪ Another sense of CONCRETE is tangible or real.

centaur Part horse, part human monster.

Minotaur Part bull, part human monster.

　　✪ Both are Greek mythical creatures.

ceremonial Concerning a ritual or ceremony. ✎ We enjoyed their CEREMONIAL dances.

ceremonious Pertaining to a concern with formalities and

27

show. ✎ We were met with CEREMONIOUS courtesy.

chalet General term for a small country house, borrowed from the decoratively trimmed huts of Switzerland.

chateau General term for any large country estate, borrowed from the houses found in the French wine regions.

chameleonic Inconstant and changeable, like chameleons, lizards that change the color of their skin. ✎ He was too CHAMELEONIC to be trustworthy.

chimerical Wildly unrealistic. ✎ Her CHIMERICAL vision of life doomed her to disappointment.

    ○ See also *mercurial*.

character What a person is.

reputation What others think a person is.

    ✎ ✎ He remained true to his CHARACTER despite the assaults on his REPUTATION.

chemotherapy The treatment of cancer or other disease with drugs.

radiotherapy The treatment of cancer or other diseases with radiation or radioactive substances.

chiefly Above all else.

largely To a great extent.

    ✎ ✎ Though he was CHIEFLY interested in teaching, he was assigned to LARGELY administrative duties.

chimpanzee An African ape.

gorilla A larger, more powerful African ape.

chintz Flower-printed polished cotton fabric. ✎ The sun room was awash in CHINTZ.

chintzy Because chintz fabrics were cheap as well as extremely popular, this slang term was coined for anything or anyone cheap. ✎ Don't be so CHINTZY!

chocolate The oily liquid derived from ground-up cacao beans.

cocoa A powder made by removing some oil from chocolate.

⊘ Both chocolate and cocoa are naturally bitter and get their sweet taste from added sugar.

churl A rude, miserly person, most commonly used in the adjective form *churlish*, but never as a verb substitute for churn: ✎ have a reputation as an unpleasant CHURL; ✎ CHURLISH behavior.

churn To stir up or to produce in quantity, not quality: ✎ CHURN up gossip; ✎ CHURN out junk novels.

cipher The mathematical symbol "0" for zero; by extension, a person without influence or value. ✎ He was a CIPHER, with as much personality as a city sparrow.

⊘ CIPHER also means a method of secret writing.

code Any system of secret or shorthand signals; more generally, a system of behavior: ✎ CODE words used to imply hidden meanings; ✎ a dress CODE.

circumference A geometric term for the distance around a circle; generally, any circular measurement. ✎ When you look at the enormous CIRCUMFERENCE of her waist, it's hard to believe she was once a size six with a twenty-two-inch waistline.

diameter A straight line stretching through a circle's center; width. ✎ The room was thirty-six feet in DIAMETER and twelve feet long.

radius A straight line from a circle's center to its edge; generally, any circular area around a central point of reference. ✎ There are three movies within a RADIUS of ten miles from our home.

classic Of established excellence.

classical Any style currently associated with an established style in art and music; strictly speaking, the creative output of the period between 1750 and 1850 identified by simplicity, harmony, and proportion.

climactic Pertaining to a climax: ✎ a CLIMACTIC event.
climatic Pertaining to climate: ✎ CLIMATIC changes.

climax A turning point that brings things to a conclusion. ✎ After an exciting CLIMAX, the writer wound things up with a happy ending.
crescendo An increase in volume; never a substitute for peak or zenith. ✎ Their applause rose in a CRESCENDO until it could be heard in the street.

cluster A gathering of a group that suggests harmony. ✎ They CLUSTERED together for warmth and comfort.
huddle A coming together to plan or conspire: ✎ a football team HUDDLING to plan its next move.

cogent Forceful or convincing. ✎ One of history's most COGENT wits is the much-quoted Anon.
pungent Having a sharp odor. ✎ A PUNGENT aroma of garlic and wine emanated from the kitchen.

cogitate To think deeply.
conjecture To guess.
✎ ✎ The more I COGITATE about it, the less I'm able to CONJECTURE about the outcome.

collaborator A partner in a creative endeavor.
ghostwriter Someone who writes a book or article that features another person's name as the author.
✎ ✎ After years as her famous husband's unsung GHOSTWRITER, she insisted on being credited as his COLLABORATOR.
○ Collaborator also has a negative meaning, specifically in reference to someone who collaborates with a person's, organization's, or country's enemies.

collate To collect and arrange items for systematic use. ✎ The wind scattered the pages they'd just COLLATED.

compile To acquire and organize facts, information, etc. into a report or book. ✎ He COMPILED his famous mother's letters into a best-selling memoir.

college A school that offers a postsecondary education and awards a baccalaureate degree such as a BA (Bachelor of Arts) or a BS (Bachelor of Science).

university An educational institution at the highest level; a network of undergraduate colleges and professional and graduate schools offering bachelor's, master's, and doctor's degrees.

colloquy A formal or informal discussion among several people. ✎ The lawyers recessed for a brief, private COLLOQUY.

soliloquy A solo speech in a play that reveals inner thoughts: ✎ Hamlet's SOLILOQUY.

cologne A mild, fragrant liquid used for scent.

eau de toilette Stronger than cologne but weaker than perfume.

perfume The scent with the highest concentration of fragrant oils, and the highest price.

compare To examine for similarities. ✎ I COMPARED their performance records.

contrast To point out differences. ✎ The CONTRAST between us is as clear as night and day.

complacent Showing satisfaction, especially with oneself. ✎ Don't be so COMPLACENT. We haven't won yet!

compliant Submissive. ✎ His once-COMPLIANT wife became a tiger after assertiveness training.

complement To make complete.

compliment To praise.

   ✎ ✎ I COMPLIMENT you on how well that scarf COM-PLEMENTS the rest of your outfit.

compose To form or make up by combining things. ✎
   The recipe is COMPOSED of just three ingredients.

comprise To include or contain all the parts of something.
   ✎ The house COMPRISES ten large rooms, three baths and a kitchen.

   ❍ While comprise as illustrated above is fine, avoid the stilted COMPRISED OF.

comprehensible Capable of being understood.
comprehensive Including or covering much.

   ✎ ✎ His report was COMPREHENSIVE and written in colorful and COMPREHENSIBLE language.

concave Curved in, like the inside of a spoon.
convex Curved out.

concert A performance by a musical group.
recital A performance by a solo performer.

concerto Classical composition for an orchestra and (usually) one instrument.
sonata Classical composition for a solo instrument or a small number of instruments without an orchestra.
symphony Classical composition for an orchestra.

concise Brevity achieved by cutting language to the bone.
pithy Brevity that's full of meaning.
succinct Brevity achieved through compressed, tight, but still flavorful language.

conclave A secret meeting; currently, anything implying secrecy. ✎ Even the press did not know about the top-level leaders' CONCLAVE.

enclave A small territory, within the boundaries of another. ✎ They lived in an ENCLAVE of privilege.

concurrent Occurring at the same time. ✎ The two conferences ran CONCURRENTLY so I had a tough choice about which one to attend.

consecutive Pertaining to events that follow each other in logical, uninterrupted order. ✎ The seminar runs for three CONSECUTIVE days, from a Thursday brunch to a Saturday night party.

successive This is like consecutive, but with an allowance for a break in the events that follow each other. ✎ The show was broadcast on four SUCCESSIVE Sundays.

concussion An injury resulting from violent impact, most commonly associated with the brain.

contusion A bruise.

condo An abbreviation for condominium, a multiple dwelling in which owners own their residences individually but share ownership and responsibility for common areas.

condop A property that consists of both condominium and cooperative units such as a building with coop apartments and condo stores.

coop An abbreviation for cooperative, a multiple dwelling providing buyers exclusive occupancy and ownership of shares in the coop corporation.

✪ A condo sale is strictly between buyer and seller; a coop sale is subject to board approval. Whichever you own, you're subject to house rules.

connote To imply a secondary meaning. ✎ To many, childhood CONNOTES innocence and fun.

denote To express meaning clearly and directly. ✎ Childhood DENOTES that stage of life between birth and independence.

consonance Melodic, pleasing sound combinations.

33

dissonance Harsh, unharmonious sound combinations.
    ✪ See also *cacophonous.*

contagious A medical term for a disease transmitted
    through personal contact.
infectious A medical term for a disease transmitted envi-
    ronmentally.
    ✪ Outside their medical framework, both words mean to
    spread: ✎ INFECTIOUS humor; ✎ CONTAGIOUS fear.

contemptible Deserving disdain.
contemptuous Expressing disdain.
    ✎ ✎ His CONTEMPTIBLE rudeness proves that he's
    CONTEMPTUOUS of common courtesy.

contentious Given to quarreling or arguing. ✎ He was
    as CONTENTIOUS as a jaybird.
sententious Given to dullness and moralizing. ✎ I slept
    through most of her SENTENTIOUS lecture.
tendentious Biased or partial to a cause. ✎ He made a
    TENDENTIOUS speech in our behalf.

continual Going on all the time but not necessarily without
    interruption. ✎ The CONTINUAL rain gave way to a few
    hours of sun each day.
continuous Nonstop, without a break. ✎ It was so hot
    last night that the air conditioner ran CONTINUOUSLY.

contretemps An unfortunate, untimely occurrence. ✎
    Their reunion stirred old memories and a whole new set
    of CONTRETEMPS.
mishap Like a contretemps, but limited to accidents. ✎
    His daydreaming led to several serious MISHAPS.

conundrum A hard-to-solve puzzle or one with no solu-
    tion. ✎ It was a philosopical CONUNDRUM for which
    they had no answer.
fulcrum Something that serves as the support on which a

lever turns. Also used figuratively. ✎ She was the FUL-CRUM of her organization: when she left, it fell into chaos.

conventional war A war that does not involve modern weapons of mass destruction.
guerrilla war A war conducted by small, irregular forces, away from enemy control points.
limited war A twentieth-century phenomenon—a war fought with specific constraints to prevent expansion into a full-scale conflict.

convince Induce someone to believe.
persuade Induce someone to act.
✎ ✎ I PERSUADED him to drop the lawsuit but he's still not CONVINCED it was the right thing to do.

copy editor A publishing employee who checks an author's manuscript for factual correctness as well as syntax errors. Copy editors are often chosen for their familiarity with a subject.
proofreader A person employed by a publisher to check for typographical and grammatical errors.
○ The *acquisitions editor* who buys an author's work rarely performs these jobs.

copyright Issued (in the U.S.) by the Copyright Office, this protects published or unpublished works of art—literature, music, plays, dances, computer programs—for a specific time period. ✎ Stephen Foster's many famous songs were not COPYRIGHTED and often earned as little as $15 each.
patent Granted (in the U.S.) by the Patent and Trademark Office, to protect an invention for a specific time. ✎ The first phonograph was built and PATENTED by Thomas Edison, but it had actually been described a year earlier by a Frenchman named Charles Cros.

trademark A term (always capitalized) registered to protect its use as a product or trade name, without time limit. ✎ Many TRADEMARKS are identified with the initials TM.

○ See also *fair use*.

cornet A shorter version of the trumpet, with a somewhat less intense and brilliant sound.
trumpet Wind instrument that uses valves to change from high to low sounds.

corpulent Large and bulky of body. ✎ Illness seemed to have shrunk his once-CORPULENT frame.
obese A medical term for excessive weight. ✎ At 180 pounds, she had definitely crossed the line between plumpness and OBESITY.

correlate To compare or connect in a systematic fashion. ✎ The study, which CORRELATED economic development and pollution, found that pollution diminishes in a growing economy.
correspond To be in accord. ✎ Do you know if this CORRESPONDS with any other studies?
corroborate To confirm or support. ✎ The study CORROBORATES several others.

credible Believable. ✎ He gave a CREDIBLE alibi.
creditable Praiseworthy. ✎ The children gave a CREDITABLE performance.
credulous Gullible. ✎ Only a CREDULOUS person would believe such a bare-faced lie.

criteria More than one standard or yardstick.
criterion A single standard or yardstick.
✎ ✎ In a survey of the main CRITERIA for friendship, trustworthiness was the one CRITERION mentioned by each respondent.

crochet To practice a venerable handicraft in which fabric is made by passing a hook through one or more loops of yarn. The number of times the yarn is looped around the hook determines the pattern.
knit To practice an ancient handicraft worked with two pointed needles and variations of knit and purl stitches.

crossbreed Any animal whose parents are of two different pure breeds.
mutt A dog whose origins can only be guessed at.
pure breed Any animal whose parents and ancestors were of the same unmixed breed.

crude Unrefined in state or style: ✎ CRUDE oil; ✎ a CRUDE but promising attempt.
rude Impolite in behavior: ✎ a RUDE remark; ✎ a RUDE interruption.

cum laude With praise.
magna cum laude With great praise.
summa cum laude With greatest praise.
   ○ Any of these Latin honors will add luster to a college diploma.

curmudgeon A grouchy person of either sex.
termagant A scold or shrewish woman.
   ✎ ✎ With *The Portable Curmudgeon*, a collection of quotations especially for grouches, an established best-seller, can *A Termagant's Tirade* be far behind?

curriculum A school's regular course of study.
syllabus The outline of a course of study.

curtain call A performer's return to the stage (nowadays mostly without actual curtains), in response to audience applause. ✎ Placido Domingo's fans once clapped for eighty-three CURTAIN CALLS.

encore An addition to the performance in response to applause. ✎ He sang several ENCORES.

customary As a matter of custom. ✎ They missed their CUSTOMARY Saturday night date.

habitual An unconscious tendency to repeat an action so that it becomes spontaneous. ✎ She's a HABITUAL liar.

cyclone A violent tropical storm with intense circular winds often accompanied by heavy rains.

hurricane A tropical cyclone, with winds over 74 m.p.h., rain, thunder, and lightning.

tornado A violent funnel-shaped whirlwind that travels a narrow path over the land.

    ❖ All these storms are often used to describe human agitation: ✎ a messy room that looks as if it had been struck by a CYCLONE; ✎ to sweep into a room like a HURRICANE or a TORNADO.

cynical The attitude of one who doubts all human goodness. ✎ His CYNICAL remarks failed to shake her belief that she could effect a change.

skeptical The attitude of one who doubts. ✎ He was SKEPTICAL about the plan's feasibility.

cynosure The focus of attention and interest.

sinecure A political job entailing special benefits and little or no work.

    ✎ ✎ The governor was the CYNOSURE of an inquiry into his administration's many SINECURES.

dais A speaker's platform that holds a number of people.

lectern A stand for the speaker's notes.

podium A speaker's or conductor's platform on top of a larger platform; also known as a rostrum.

damp Slightly wet. ✎ Her hair was still DAMP from showering.

dank Wet and smelly. ✎ The hostages were held in a cold, DANK cellar.

debate To participate in an argument or discussion.

deliberate To determine a result; to consider.

✎ ✎ They DEBATED hotly whether to DELIBERATE the matter further or adjourn for lunch.

debut A first appearance.

premiere A first performance.

✎ ✎ She made her Broadway DEBUT in the PREMIERE performance of a new musical.

deceitful Deliberately dishonest or false. ✎ Don't be taken in by her DECEITFUL friendliness!

deceptive Misleading or confusing. ✎ His comic looks are DECEPTIVE. He's really a very serious person.

deface To damage or disfigure the surface of something. ✎ Graffiti DEFACED the mayor's statue.

defile To make dirty or pollute. ✎ Her reputation was DEFILED by rumors. ✎ Chemicals DEFILED the river.

defective Faulty: ✎ a DEFECTIVE appliance.

deficient Lacking: ✎ DEFICIENT in nourishment.

definitely With certainty. ✎ I'll DEFINITELY be there.

definitive Final and not subject to change. ✎ That's a DEFINITIVE offer. Take it or leave it.

defuse Literally, to disable an explosive device; figuratively, to lower tension.

39

diffuse To spread out or intermix.

✎ ✎ His humor and calm DEFUSED the tensions aroused by the reports DIFFUSED by his enemies.

deign To do something in a condescending rather than a willing manner; to lower oneself to do it.
disdain Verb or noun for scorn.

✎ ✎ At first she DISDAINED his offer. When she did DEIGN to accept, it was too late.

dejected In low spirits. ✎ They were DEJECTED by the team's loss.
disconsolate Too dejected to be consoled. ✎ His death left her DISCONSOLATE.

demagogue One who rises to power by appealing to people's prejudices.
despot A tyrannical ruler.

✎ ✎ DEMAGOGUES usually turn into DESPOTS.

deplete To use up. ✎ Overwork DEPLETED his energies.
depreciate To lose value as a result of use or aging. ✎ The property's value DEPRECIATED by 30 percent.

desert An arid land: ✎ the Sahara DESERT.
dessert Fruit, cheese, or sweets served at the end of a meal—originating from the act of clearing the table to make room for dessert.

❂ In the phrase *to get your just deserts*, *deserts* is pronounced like *dessert* and spelled as shown. The phrase means to get what you deserve.

desultory Lacking in direction; aimless. ✎ After a few DESULTORY attempts to master the game, he stopped playing.
negligent To be remiss or careless. ✎ He tends to be NEGLIGENT about details.

negligible Too small or unimportant to warrant serious attention or concern. ✎ In the overall scheme of things, his faults are NEGLIGIBLE.

detergent A synthetic cleanser, most commonly made from petroleum byproducts.
soap An organic cleanser combining fat and alkali.

detract Take away from. ✎ Worry about her sick child DETRACTED from her joy in winning the award.
distract To draw attention to something else. ✎ His nervous gestures DISTRACTED me from what he had to say.

diagnosis The process of identifying a problem: ✎ a DIAGNOSIS of cancer; ✎ a DIAGNOSIS of recession.
prognosis The process of predicting what to expect from the diagnosed problem: ✎ a PROGNOSIS for full recovery; ✎ a gloomy PROGNOSIS.

dialect The form of a language as it is spoken in a particular region: ✎ a mountain DIALECT.
jargon Language particular to special interests: ✎ sports JARGON; ✎ technological JARGON.
vernacular The distinctive, everyday expressions of a country's or region's language: ✎ American English as opposed to British English; ✎ southern or New England idioms.

diastolic pressure The lower and more important of the two numbers in blood pressure tests, the one that measures the pressure of the blood against the artery walls when the heart is at rest.
systolic pressure The higher test number that reports the blood's pressure against the artery walls when the heart contracts.
 ✎ ✎ SYSTOLIC PRESSURE is always higher than DIASTOLIC PRESSURE because blood is pushed through the artery faster at the peak of the heart's pumping action.

dictionary A book that gives the meaning and pronunciation of the words of a language.

glossary A collection of specialized terms and their definitions; not a complete dictionary.

⊙ See also, *atlas*.

didactic Instructive or moralistic. ✎ His lecture was more DIDACTIC than entertaining.

dogmatic With an air of conviction. ✎ I had no argument with which to counter her DOGMATIC declaration.

differentiated cancer Cancer in which there is a clear differentiation between malignant cells and cells from the source, such as lymph node cells and malignant cells in a breast.

nondifferentiated cancer Cancer in which the cells at the source of a cancer's origin overpower cells elsewhere.

⊙ As a general rule, differentiated cancer cells are closer to the original normal tissue and therefore are easier to treat.

diffidence Lack of confidence.

indifference Lack of concern.

✎ ✎ I tried to hide my DIFFIDENCE behind a facade of INDIFFERENCE.

dignitary Someone of high rank or in a high position. ✎ The governor was one of many DIGNITARIES who attended the opening ceremonies.

luminary Someone of great stature in his or her field. ✎ The school's most successful fund raising event is an annual concert at which the student orchestra plays with a LUMINARY from the professional music world.

dilemma A puzzling question or situation, usually requiring a decision or choice between two equally balanced alternatives. ✎ Like many working mothers, Mary was faced with the DILEMMA of choosing between a demanding job that would give her less time with her children, or working fewer hours in a less interesting job.

predicament A difficult or unpleasant situation that may entail an element of danger. ✎ They found themselves in a PREDICAMENT every driver can sympathize with: A deserted country road at night, pouring rain and a stalled engine.

✎ ✎ His DILEMMA was to find a way to extricate himself from his current PREDICAMENT as quickly as possible.

dinosaur Extinct, lizard-like and sometimes enormously large creatures; used figuratively for anything or anyone outmoded. ✎ The family farm is often regarded as on its way to becoming a DINOSAUR.

ultrasaurus One of the most recently discovered dinosaur types, said to be more than five stories high.

diplomacy The skill needed to approach situations requiring tact. ✎ The outspoken official was hardly a model of DIPLOMACY.

tact The ability to act and speak without giving offense, no matter how sensitive or difficult a situation. ✎ Personal assistants to famous people are masters of the TACTFUL brushoff.

director The person with artistic responsibility for turning a movie or play script into a finished production.

producer The fundraiser for a play or movie who also oversees hiring and all business transactions.

discover To find something that exists. ✎ Columbus set sail around the world and DISCOVERED America.

invent To create something new. ✎ Alexander Graham Bell INVENTED the telephone.

discreet Showing a sense of appropriateness or modesty.

discrete Consisting of distinctly separate things.

✎ ✎ It's DISCREET to keep one's office and personal problems DISCRETE.

43

❂ Confusion tends to arise from the fact that both words share one pronunciation.

discriminating Discerning or selective. ✎ They cater to highly DISCRIMINATING customers.

discriminatory Unfair or biased. ✎ Your record as an employer is blatantly DISCRIMINATORY!

discursive Pertaining to a discussion or talk that meanders from one subject to another.

expansive Pertaining to ease in communicating.

✎ ✎ He was in a DISCURSIVE mood, and more EXPAN-SIVE about his past than ever before.

disinterested Lacking bias. ✎ He's a DISINTERESTED witness, with no personal axe to grind.

uninterested Lacking interest (tied to boredom). ✎ I'm UNINTERESTED in their personal squabbles.

dismantle To break down or disassemble. ✎ She DIS-MANTLED my arguments like a camper packing up his tent.

dissemble To conceal motives or feelings behind a pre-tense. ✎ He DISSEMBLED so well that none of us guessed at his despair.

diuretic Something that causes urination.

emetic Something that causes vomiting.

diurnal Concerning the daytime.

nocturnal Concerning nighttime.

divers More than one; various. ✎ We could not keep track of her DIVERS acquaintances, friends, and lovers.

diverse Different and distinct. ✎ She's had a DIVERSE and fascinating life.

dock The water beside or between piers, or the pier itself;

also what you do when you land a boat.

pier A platform extending from the shore, over water.

wharf A ship's landing place.

dolphin A small-toothed cetacean or marine animal, star of aquarium and marine shows, recognizable by its bearlike snout.

manatee A huge, seal-like vegetarian mammal found in Florida's shallow waters—where it is in danger of extinction because of damage caused by boats.

porpoise Another popular cetacean, but smaller and with a blunt, rounded snout.

DOS Acronym for the Microsoft Corporation's disk operating system used to manage computer files.

Windows A newer operating system. It hides DOS-typed commands behind a graphic facade and is worked by pointing at symbols or menu items and clicking an electronic mouse device.

douse To pour water over.

dowse To search for water with a divining rod.

each other Used of two people.

one another Used of more than two.

    ✎ ✎ After he and I got through arguing with EACH OTHER, Tom and Jerry arrived and we all ended up shouting at ONE ANOTHER.

eccentric Odd in attitudes or behavior. ✎ They seemed to enjoy their ECCENTRIC living arrangements.

erratic Like eccentric, but also irregular or uneven.

✎ His paintings, though brilliant, were produced at ER-RATIC intervals between bouts of drinking.

ectomorph A tall, thin person.
endomorph A short, fat person.
  ○ Both derive from the language of psychology.

edge city An urban center with most of the attributes of a "regular" city or "downtown" (employment, stores, entertainment), but spread out around highways and malls instead of streets.
exurb A residential community within commuting distance of a city, but further away than a suburb and with more of the attributes of a town.
  ○ See also *town*.

effeminate Displaying or expressing the soft qualities associated with women. ✎ He was a big, brawny guy with a surprisingly EFFEMINATE voice.
effete Worn out; lacking vigor. ✎ We were shocked to see this EFFETE shadow of the once-great star.

effervescent Bubbling with enthusiasm. ✎ She was as EFFERVESCENT as a puppy at a picnic.
evanescent Disappearing as instantly as vapor. ✎ Her fame was as EVANESCENT as a rainbow.

efficacious Producing a desired outcome. ✎ It was an EFFICACIOUS solution to a ticklish problem.
efficient Producing results without wasted time or effort. ✎ By being EFFICIENT, he's able to sell his handcrafted pots at fair prices.

effulgence Something that shines brilliantly. ✎ They were awestruck by the sunset's EFFULGENCE.
effusion An unbounded outpouring of words or feelings. ✎ His few healing words were more meaningful than all their EFFUSIONS.

e.g. Latin abbreviation for *exempli gratia* or "for example."
i.e. Latin abbreviation for *id est*, meaning "that is."
 ○ Though these Latinisms are popular, using the English words will avoid any possibility of confusion.

ego The conscious self known as "I."
id The instinctive or primal part of the psyche.
libido The sensual link to the psyche.

egregious Extremely bad: ✎ an EGREGIOUS error; ✎ EGREGIOUS misbehavior.
exiguous Extremely meager, scanty. ✎ An EXIGUOUS wage; ✎ a plot of land too EXIGUOUS for a large building; ✎ a town with only enough job opportunities for an EXIGUOUS population.

elegy A funeral song or poem: ✎ Gray's famous "Elegy."
eulogy Words of praise for someone, usually at a funeral or memorial service. ✎ There wasn't a dry eye after his teenage son's eloquent EULOGY.

elicit To obtain information. ✎ He ELICITED the truth with patient and skillful questioning.
solicit To seek out or plead for. ✎ Their aim is to SOLICIT funds to elect more women senators.

elusive Persons, creatures, or ideas that are hard to pin down. ✎ On the presidential campaign trail, the truth is often ELUSIVE.
furtive Secretive in behavior. ✎ She was as FURTIVE as a chipmunk.

emaciated So thin as to look ill. ✎ She looked EMACIATED after the month-long hunger strike.
emasculated Robbed of strength. ✎ He seemed EMASCULATED by his long illness.

emigrant One who leaves one place for another.

47

immigrant One who has arrived in a new country.
migrant Anyone who moves from place to place.

eminent Exceptional in ability, virtue, or prominence: ✎
an EMINENT scholar; ✎ to be eminent in one's field.
immanent Existing in; inherent. ✎ An IMMANENT tendency toward moodiness.
imminent Near or immediately at hand: ✎ in IMMINENT danger.

Emmy The annual award presented to outstanding achievers in the television industry.
Grammy The record industry's most prestigious annual awards, encompassing all musical styles. It's named after the first popular phonograph, the gramophone.
Obie The off-Broadway counterpart of the Emmy awards.
Oscar The annual award for movie industry achievers, the one that inspired all other performing arts honors.
Tony The annual award for achievers in the theater, named for director-producer Antoinette Perry.

emulsifier A food additive to keep ingredients mixed and held together. ✎ EMULSIFIERS give ice cream its creamy texture.
preservative A food additive, such as salt, that prevents spoilage caused by the growth of bacteria.

encomium Formal praise. ✎ The president's ENCOMIUM crowned the dinner given in his honor.
opprobrium The disgrace suffered by wrongdoers. ✎ The OPPROBRIUM heaped on him for his dishonesty forced him to resign.

endemic Common to a particular locale or population; often, but not always, a physical or social disease. ✎ Homelessness has become ENDEMIC to big cities all over the world.

epidemic A rapidly spreading disease and, by extension, anything that spreads rapidly. ✎ The closing of two local plants caused an unemployment EPIDEMIC.

pandemic Pertaining to a widespread epidemic and, by extension, anything general or universal. ✎ As the recession widened, consumer caution became PANDEMIC.

endless An abundance of time, with no end in sight: ✎ an ENDLESS wait; ✎ an ENDLESS summer.

innumerable Too many to count: ✎ to be blessed with INNUMERABLE friends.

endnotes Explanatory notes at the end of each chapter or after the final chapter.

footnotes Explanatory notes at the bottom of the page where the text to which they pertain appears.

⊙ Numbers in subscript or superscript in the text serve as cross-references to both kinds of notes.

entomology The study of insects.

etymology The study of words.

entrenched Firmly fixed.

inchoate Newly begun.

✎ ✎ As the INCHOATE group that split off from the ENTRENCHED party gained strength and support, the Old Guard began to take notice.

envy Feelings of discontent or desire aroused by other people's good fortune or achievement. ✎ Their house was the ENVY of the whole neighborhood.

jealousy A more spiteful kind of envy that begrudges another's good fortune; also, the desire to guard something carefully for fear of losing it: ✎ To be tortured with JEALOUSY; ✎ To be JEALOUS of one's rights.

eon A period of long and indefinite duration, often used figuratively for something too long ago to remember.

era   A long period identified with important developments. ✎ ✎ We grew up in the big swing band ERA. To someone born in the sixties, that's EONS ago.

epic   Traditionally, a long narrative poem focusing on heroic deeds, like the *Iliad*; currently, any literary or dramatic work on a grand scale.

saga   A story involving many characters and scenes, often advertised as being of epic proportions.

epigram   A short, witty saying: ✎ A wise man knows everything; a shrewd one, everybody.

epigraph   An inscription on a stone, monument or building; also a motto or quotation at the beginning of a book or chapter. ✎ Oliver Wendell Holmes and Mark Twain provided the EPIGRAPHS at the beginning of this book.

epitaph   An inscription on a tomb. ✎ Sarah Smith—beloved wife, mother, and daughter.

epithet   A word or phrase to characterize a person or express scorn. ✎ A descriptive title like Catherine the Great is one kind of EPITHET; an invective phrase such as "he looked like the little man on a wedding cake" (about Thomas E. Dewey), is another.

equinox   The time when night and day are the same length, no matter where on earth you live.

solstice   The longest (June) and shortest (December) daytime periods in the northern hemisphere; also known as summer solstice and winter solstice.

equitable   Characterized by fairness: ✎ The settlement gave each heir an EQUITABLE share of the estate.

equivocal   Characterized by evasion or ambiguity. ✎ The president remains disturbingly EQUIVOCAL about an issue on which he should be taking a firm stand. —

erotic   Sexually arousing. ✎ The movie was X-rated because it contained many EROTIC scenes.

esoteric Appealing to specialized interests. ✎ The movie is too ESOTERIC to appeal to a large audience.

exotic Strange and fascinating because it's different. ✎ The story unfolds against an EXOTIC background.

estate A person's entire assets; legally, the extent of an owner's rights to and use of property.

trust A legal title to property held by a trustee for a beneficiary. By general extension, anything put into someone's custody or care.

✎✎ His ESTATE included several houses and a college TRUST fund for each of his grandchildren.

et al. Latin for "and others." ✎ The paper was presented by Smith, Conners, *et al.*

etc. Latin abbreviation for *et cetera*, meaning "and other things." ✎ The play won many awards: best musical, best direction, etc.

○ As with other foreign abbreviations, the surest road to clarity is to use the English words.

euphemism An expression used instead of another that might give offense: ✎ "comb my hair" instead of "going to the bathroom;" ✎ "pass away" for "die."

solecism A grammatical misuse: ✎ ain't; ✎ it don't matter.

ewe A female sheep.

ram A male sheep.

exacerbate To make worse: ✎ to EXACERBATE a situation.

exasperate To annoy: ✎ to EXASPERATE somone enough to provoke a fight.

exception Something removed from the norm. ✎ I'll make an EXCEPTION for today only and let you go.

exemption To excuse from an obligation. ✎ Senior citizens were given a tax EXEMPTION.

51

excise To delete anything considered unnecessary. ✑
They EXCISED all out-of-date material.
expurgate To delete any unacceptable material. ✑ They
published an EXPURGATED school edition.

excursion Any short trip for pleasure or relaxation. ✑
They went on an EXCURSION to the zoo.
expedition A trip with a specific purpose. ✑ What did
you buy on your shopping EXPEDITION?

exhausting Tiring.
exhaustive Very thorough.
✑ ✑ EXHAUSTIVE housecleaning is EXHAUSTING.

exhort To urge or plead. ✑ She EXHORTED them to act.
press Like exhort, but with a connotation of pressure. ✑ Un-
daunted by their refusal, she continued to PRESS for action.

expedient In a timely and convenient manner: ✑ We found
it EXPEDIENT to work with an *ad hoc* committee.
expeditious In a speedy, prompt manner. ✑ The hearing
was brought to an EXPEDITIOUS conclusion.

explicit Clearly and definitely stated or shown. ✑ A
movie with such EXPLICIT violence should be X-rated.
implicit Suggested rather than stated. ✑ I didn't need to
have a gun pointed at me to recognize the IMPLICIT threat
in his remarks.

extant In existence. ✑ Few journalists EXTANT are more
admired than she.
extinct No longer alive or active. ✑ Their expedition led
them to artifacts from a long EXTINCT culture.

extemporaneous Without rehearsal or preparation. ✑
He added a number of EXTEMPORANEOUS remarks to his
prepared statement.
extraneous A reference in a speech or article not pertaining

to the basic idea, usually with a negative connotation.  We could have done without his EXTRANEOUS commentary.

extrovert An outgoing, sociable individual.
introvert An extrovert's opposite.

F

factious Divided; creating division.  Politicians are a FACTIOUS lot.  Abortion is a FACTIOUS issue.
fractious One who's unruly or irritable.  It's hard to have a reasonable discussion with such a FRACTIOUS bunch.

fade in Movie (and TV) term for an effect in which the image gradually appears from complete darkness.
fade out An effect where the screen image gradually fades to complete darkness.
○ Both terms are also used more generally.  Over the years, he faded in and out of our lives.

fair use The right to use portions of copyrighted text; copyright rules, which vary according to the source and application, are strictest with respect to small-circulation publications and songs.
public domain Creative properties (novels, poems, songs, computer programs), without copyright protection and thus not subject to royalties.
○ See also, *copyright.*

farrago A mixture or medley:  a FARRAGO of ideas.
fracas A disorderly quarrel:  a schoolyard FRACAS.
 The FRACAS that broke up the celebration, can be attributed to a FARRAGO of absurd circumstances.

53

farther Use this to refer to distance or space. ✎ She ran FARTHER than anyone else.

further Use this to show an addition or advantage or to refer to degree, quantity, or time. ✎ Your contribution will FURTHER our cause. ✎ Their FURTHER successes fulfilled her high hopes after that brilliant debut.

fauna Animals in general.
flora Plants in general.
✎ ✎ We discovered a wealth of FAUNA and FLORA.

faze To perturb.
frazzle To exhaust or wear out.
✎ ✎ Hard work doesn't FAZE me, but office politics do FRAZZLE my nerves.

feckless Ineffective. ✎ After the last candidate's FECKLESS performance, the party was badly in need of a winner.
fecund Fertile, fruitful—either literal or figurative. ✎ His FECUND imagination was the source for dozens of novels.

felicitous Anything particularly appropriate to a situation: ✎ to break the ice with a few FELICITOUS jokes.
solicitous Showing concern or eagerness: ✎ to be SOLICITOUS about someone's welfare; ✎ SOLICITOUS about a friend's difficulties.

felony A serious crime. ✎ White collar crime is a FELONY subject to a jail sentence.
misdemeanor A lesser crime. ✎ Violating a municipal ordinance is a MISDEMEANOR subject to a fine or at most a year in jail.
❍ See also, *grand larceny.*

femur The thighbone, between the pelvis and the knee.
fibula The outer part of the lower leg.
tibia The shinbone, which extends from the back of the knee to the ankle.

ferret To drive out or uncover.
forage To search for food or any kind of supplies.
    ✪ You FERRET *out* and FORAGE *for*.

fetish An irrational attachment. ✎ Her constant cleaning became a FETISH.
penchant A decided taste for something. ✎ Their earnings hardly support their PENCHANT for high living.

fewer Use this for a reduction of countable things. ✎ FEWER tourists came this year than last.
less Use this for a reduction in anything measured or in degree, quantity, or extent. ✎ There's LESS tourism during a recession.
    ✎ ✎ To weigh LESS, consume FEWER calories.

field A tract of open land, especially fertile land; by extension, any area of endeavor. ✎ Young people are scrambling to find new FIELDS of opportunity.
meadow Any land where grass and flowers grow.

figuratively In a symbolic, nonliteral sense.
literally In actual fact, without exaggeration.
virtually More in a manner of speaking than in actual fact. ✎ ✎ ✎ Because they were LITERALLY raised like brothers, they were VIRTUALLY inseparable. FIGURATIVELY speaking, you might say they're as close as two peas in a pod.

financial Pertaining to money. ✎ The company slashed jobs to extricate themselves from their FINANCIAL bind.
fiscal Pertaining to public money. ✎ The governor's FISCAL policies were under attack.

first edition All copies of a book using all of its original plates. The plates are used until the book is revised.
first printing A book's first press run.
    ✎ ✎ After a FIRST PRINTING of 10,000 copies and nu-

merous subsequent printings, a second updated and expanded EDITION was published.

flaunt To show off. ✎ She lived by the motto: If you've got it, FLAUNT it.

flout To openly and defiantly disregard. ✎ She took more pleasure in FLOUTING than obeying conventions.

floppy disk A magnetically coated disk used to store computer files. ✎ Many people think of 3.5" FLOPPY DISKS as hard because they're inside a hard case.

hard disk A disk of large capacity that is generally inside the computer although external hard disk drives are also available. ✎ HARD DISKS generally hold at least twenty megabytes.

flotsam Material from a wreck that floats around.

jetsam Material thrown overboard at sea and washed ashore. Jetsam is rarely used alone, unlike its verb form, to jettison, which means to toss out.

○ Flotsam and jetsam, or flotsam by itself, currently refers to anything or anyone drifting about like a ship's waste materials.

flounder To muddle along. ✎ Until he met her, he FLOUNDERED from one relationship to another.

founder What happens if you stop floundering and fail completely. ✎ Their initial closeness notwithstanding, their romance finally FOUNDERED.

fog A thick, hard-to-see-through mist; in everyday terms, a state that blocks clear thinking: ✎ I can't remember what happened. I was in a FOG that day.

mist Condensed vapor that can dim one's view, but not as completely as a fog; also used in the sense of not looking at things too sharply. ✎ She was caught up in a sentimental MIST.

forego Go before. ✎ As explained in the FOREGOING para-
graphs . . .

forgo To give up or abstain from: ✎ FORGO a treat.

foreword A book's introduction, usually by someone other
than the author. ✎ A FOREWORD by a well-known person adds prestige to a book.

forward A direction. ✎ The car moved FORWARD.

preface The author's or speaker's introduction. ✎ I'd like
to PREFACE my speech with a tribute to our host.

forked lightning Lightning visible as a jagged streak.

heat lightning Lightning visible as a series of flashes.
    ✪ All lightning is a discharge of electricity from one
cloud to another or between a cloud and the earth.

fortuitous Happening by chance. ✎ It was FORTUITOUS
that someone came along to help.

fortunate Lucky. ✎ You were FORTUNATE that no one
was in the other car.

fractional Of a fraction or anything very small. ✎ The
difference was FRACTIONAL, having no effect on the result.

infinitesimal Even smaller than fractional. ✎ The chance
that it's a malignancy is truly INFINITESIMAL.

freefall A fall without a safety device such as a parachute;
by extension, any uncontrolled situation.

shortfall A deficit, with no connection to the unexpected.

windfall Once a word for the branches blown down from
the trees and collected for firewood and now any unexpected gain or advantage.
    ✎ ✎ ✎ The business was in a FREEFALL after suffer-
ing one SHORTFALL after another. Only a WINDFALL of
orders could turn things around.

fringe benefits Nontaxable employee advantages or

perks, from free education to free trips.

stock options A specific fringe benefit—the right to buy company stock at a fixed price.

frog A small cold-blooded animal, living in or out of the water. Its croaking voice has given rise to the expression "a frog in one's throat" for hoarseness.

toad A froglike earthbound animal that's considered so ugly that it's become a synonym for an extremely unattractive person.

frown To wrinkle one's forehead thoughtfully or disapprovingly.

scowl An extremely angry frown.

✎ ✎ When he realized he'd been duped his puzzled FROWN deepened into a SCOWL.

fulsome Sickeningly excessive or disgusting, unconnected to "fullness" as in abundance. ✎ You're wise not to take his FULSOME praise seriously.

noisome Another adjective that sounds like something it isn't, noisome refers to anything harmful or offensive. ✎ The NOISOME reek of the sanitation truck sent us running for cover.

furor Widespread uproar or extreme excitement.

fury Violence pertaining to weather or mood.

✎ ✎ The FURY with which she defended her position caused quite a FUROR among the rest of the staff.

G

gaffer An old man. Also "movie-ese" for the chief electrician for a movie.

grip "Movie-ese" for any manual laborer on a movie set, who may perform such tasks as building, moving, loading, and carrying equipment. A major production has many grips, and Hollywood "insiders" don't leave a movie until the chief grip's credit rolls by.

gambit A specific opening move in chess, now applied to any carefully planned strategy. ✎ His GAMBIT for outwitting his opponent worked, but only once.

gamut Originally, the whole musical scale, and now anything expressing a complete range. ✎ The play ran the GAMUT from hilarity to tragedy.

gastroenterologist A physician for disorders of the digestive system.

gerontologist A physician for diseases and problems of old age.

genius One with exceptional natural ability. ✎ Einstein was a mathematical GENIUS.

prodigy A child demonstrating extraordinary talent at a very early age. ✎ A true PRODIGY'S talents do not disappear with age.

German measles Common name for rubella, a disease especially dangerous for pregnant women.

measles A highly infectious virus characterized by high fever and a red rash; also known by its medical name, rubeola.

glare To look angrily: ✎ to GLARE fiercely.

leer To look slyly or lustfully: ✎ a knowing LEER; ✎ a lascivious LEER.

stare To look very intently: ✎ a persistent STARE; ✎ a thoughtful STARE; ✎ a lingering STARE.

go gold Of a record, to achieve certified sales of 500,000.

go platinum To achieve certified sales of 1 million.

○ These sales figures, certified by the Record Industry Association of America, were adjusted downward in 1990 from 1 million for gold and 2 million for platinum.

gospel   Music first heard in black American churches during the days of slavery.

soul   Gospel plus a touch of the blues and pop, introduced in the 1940s by pianist Ray Charles.

gourmand   One who loves food in large quantities; a glutton. ✎ The restaurant's portions were large enough to satisfy any GOURMAND.

gourmet   A food and wine lover more concerned with quality than quantity. ✎ The restaurant serves GOURMET meals fit for the most discerning tastes.

grand larceny   Theft of property worth more than the sum that constitutes petty larceny.

petty larceny   A lesser theft.

○ While the theft of a jacket or twenty-five dollars would generally fall into the petty larceny classification, the dividing line that establishes theft classification is arbitrarily determined by individual states.

○ See also *felony*.

grapple   To struggle or take hold of physically or mentally: ✎ to GRAPPLE with changes in society; ✎ to GRAPPLE with an attacker.

grope   Struggle hesitantly to find one's way, physically (with one's hands), or mentally: ✎ to GROPE around in the dark; ✎ to GROPE desperately for a solution.

○ The use of one's hands to grope, has led to grope's slang usage for touching or fondling someone in a sexual way.

grave   A burial place, usually in the ground.

tomb   A burial structure.

greenhouse effect The warming of the earth's surface and lower atmosphere caused when solar radiation is converted to heat and trapped in the atmosphere by certain gasses.

ozone depletion Another modern health hazard. It's caused by the failure of the ozone layer in the stratosphere to block all the sun's harmful ultraviolet radiation.

grisly Something gruesome: 🖎 a GRISLY murder.

grizzly Something gray or speckled with gray: 🖎 a GRIZZLY beard.

gross earnings Earnings before expenses are deducted.

net earnings Earnings after expenses are deducted.
🖎 🖎 His GROSS EARNINGS were $100,000, but expenses reduced the NET to $25,000.

H

halcyon days Calm and peaceful days, named after a bird of the sea once believed to have the power to calm the winds and waves. 🖎 Ah for the HALCYON days of childhood vacations!

salad days The days when you're young and innocent, as first used in Shakespeare's Cleopatra: 🖎 "My SALAD DAYS, when I was green in judgment . . ."

hamentaschen A triangular pastry, often filled with poppy seeds, eaten during Purim to commemorate Esther's deliverance of the Persian Jews from a murderous official named Haman.

latkes Potato pancakes, eaten especially during Hanukkah, the festival of lights that commemorates the re-dedication of the Temple of Jerusalem.

61

Hebrew A semitic language, once used only in Jewish textbooks and other religious contexts, but currently the official language of the state of Israel.

Yiddish A Germanic language spoken by Jews from many countries. Its many colorful expressions have been adopted by people of many faiths and backgrounds.

hedonist One who lives for pleasure.

stoic One who calmly and uncomplainingly endures difficulties and pain.

heterogeneous Made up of mixed or unlike parts.

homogeneous Made up of like parts.

✎ ✎ New York City is a HETEROGENEOUS city with many HOMOGENEOUS enclaves.

high-density lipoprotein The declogging cholesterol that fights heart disease, known as HDLs.

low-density lipoprotein The cholesterol that clogs arteries, including the heart's, known as LDLs.

✪ Most tests measure the total cholesterol in the blood, which should be no more than 200.

homograph A word spelled like another but pronounced differently: ✎ the *row* (rhymes with go) your seats are in at the theater and a marital *row* (rhymes with cow).

homonym A word spelled and pronounced like another but different in meaning: ✎ a ship's *bow* and to take a *bow*.

homophone A word that sounds like another but that differs in both meaning and spelling: ✎ To *brake* at the light and the plate you *break*.

✪ See also *oxymoron*.

honorarium A payment made in a situation where no legal fee is involved. ✎ Our group has never had an official budget for speakers's fees, though we do manage to pay a very small HONORARIUM when a distinguished visiting speaker comes to town.

stipend A regular payment such as an allowance. ✎ The former millionaire's old associates provided him with a hundred-dollar-a-week STIPEND.

horrendous An informal adjective for anything awful or horrifying. ✎ The play was so HORRENDOUS we were tempted to walk out before the end.

stupendous Also informal, but meaning amazing or great. ✎ It was a STUPENDOUS achievement.

hospice A word resurrected from its long-ago use as a resting place for travelers to describe a special hospital for dying patients.

hostel Inexpensive lodging, once mostly for young people (youth hostel) but currently also popular with retirees (Elderhostel).

hot tub A combination sauna and whirlpool.

sauna A dry heat bath.

whirlpool A bath in which hot water is propelled with a swirling motion, also known as a Jacuzzi (a trademark of the Jacuzzi company).

hovercraft A speedy boat that rides on a cushion of air.

hydrofoil Another speedy boat. It has a raised hull that "flies" across rivers, harbors, and other bodies of water.

ice cream Popular dessert made from milk products, gelatin, sweeteners, and flavorings, containing 10 to 20 percent butterfat.

sherbet The nonfat but sweeter alternative to ice cream, made from fruit juice, sweeteners, egg whites, and milk or water; also known as sorbet.

idiosyncrasy An unusual way of behaving. ✎ Colorful wigs were just one of her style IDIOSYNCRASIES.

peccadillo A minor fault or offense. ✎ He referred to his wife's habit of fibbing as a PECCADILLO.

immerse To plunge deeply into liquid or an interesting activity. ✎ They IMMERSED themselves totally in their new business.

infuse To introduce or penetrate as if by pouring or soaking. ✎ The new manager INFUSED new life into the dying business. ✎ She was a teacher who INFUSED her student with enthusiasm.

immunity State of being exempt or protected from anything troublesome, such as a disease. ✎ More than a million automobiles are stolen annually, and rental cars are not IMMUNE.

impunity Also a state of exemption, but specifically related to punishment. ✎ Experts fear a 1991 court ruling on insider trading may allow investors to profit from such illegal dealings with IMPUNITY.

imply To hint. ✎ Although she didn't say so, she IMPLIED that her job was at risk.

infer To draw a conclusion. ✎ I INFER from her attitude that she's prepared to deal with whatever happens.

insinuate To hint, usually with a negative connotation; also to craftily work oneself in. ✎ Tom INSINUATED that she might be fired for incompetence, not because of overall cutbacks. ✎ He failed in his attempt to INSINUATE himself into her good graces.

impracticable Not capable of being done.

impractical Not sensible or prudent.

✎ ✎ Even if his plan had been less IMPRACTICABLE,

he's much too IMPRACTICAL to see it through.

inane Foolish, empty-headed. ✎ No one paid attention to his INANE chatter.

supercilious A haughty, conceited look or manner. ✎ Take that SUPERCILIOUS look off your face!

incandescent Intensely bright and clear. ✎ Her language is INCANDESCENT and often funny.

iridescent Shimmering with colors like a rainbow. ✎ An IRIDESCENT glow brightened the dark gym.

incongruous Jarringly inconsistent.
inconsonant Not in accord.
✎ ✎ It seemed INCONGRUOUS for two people with such INCONSONANT tastes to marry successfully.

incredible Implausible and thus hard to believe.
incredulous Showing disbelief.
✎ ✎ I was INCREDULOUS that he thought I would swallow his totally INCREDIBLE alibi.

indeterminate Not possible to estimate precisely. ✎ At this point, the opening date is INDETERMINATE.

interminable Seemingly endless. ✎ It took them an INTERMINABLE time to reach a verdict.

indolent Inclined to avoid exertion. ✎ If a sheet of music fell from the bed on which the talented but INDOLENT Rossini composed his operas, he would write something else rather than retrieve it.

lethargic Sluggish, dull behavior. ✎ The heat wave made us all too LETHARGIC to do much.

infraction The breaking of a rule or law. ✎ He wound up in jail even though it was a minor INFRACTION.

infringement An intrusion on someone's right or property. ✎ That's an INFRINGEMENT of my basic rights!

ingenious Resourceful or inventive.
ingenuous Open and aboveboard and often naive.
✎ ✎ He was too INGENUOUS to protect his INGENIOUS ideas properly.

initiate To start something: ✎ to INITIATE a new system; ✎ to INITIATE a movement.
instigate To incite others to act: ✎ to INSTIGATE a student revolt.

insidious Happening or spreading subtly and dangerously. ✎ The INSIDIOUS rumors mounted in intensity.
invidious Actions, often evil, that offend or arouse ill will. ✎ The police made every effort to stem the INVIDIOUS wave of hate crimes.

intelligently With knowledge and sense.
✎ ✎ He writes INTELLIGENTLY, but with that wispy voice he's not an INTELLIGIBLE speaker.
intelligible Understandable.

intergalactic Between the galaxies (collections of millions of stars bound together by gravity).
interplanetary Between planets.
interstellar Between stars.

intern A recent graduate of a medical school on the staff of a hospital but still under supervision.
resident What the intern becomes when he trains in a specialty.

intractable Hard to manage, stubborn. ✎ It was an INTRACTABLE problem, defying every solution.
intransigent Uncompromising in one's position. ✎ Nothing short of an earthquake would change his INTRANSIGENT stance.

inveigh To argue or speak out loudly. ✎ He INVEIGHED against the press corps with his usual zest.

inveigle To tempt, entice, or persuade. Despite his promises he could not INVEIGLE her to join him.

invertebrate Species without a backbone or spinal column, like clams and worms.
vertebrate Species with a backbone, like fish, dogs, birds, or humans.

irony Words that convey the opposite of their literal meaning; or events contrary to what was or might have been expected. "That's about as easy as shoveling snow with a teaspoon," is an IRONIC way to say that something is impossible to do. The IRONY of the novelist's first real success is that she spent years on her earlier failed novels, while she completed her best seller in just one month.
satire To ridicule, or to expose human follies and social ills with irony, sarcasm, or ridicule. The play is a razor-sharp SATIRE of the political process.

its Possessive of the pronoun it. Hate raised ITS ugly head.
it's Contraction for *it is* or *it has*. IT'S a must to know the difference between ITS and IT'S.

J

jam Sweet, thick spread made from fruit pulp and sugar.
jelly Sweet spread made from fruit juice and sugar.

jet engine Any engine that obtains its force by ejecting a stream of gaseous combustion products, with the surrounding atmosphere providing the oxygen needed for its fuel combustion.

rocket engine Like a jet-propelled engine except that the oxygen is not supplied by the atmosphere.

jockey To maneuver for an advantageous position.  She JOCKEYED herself into the top spot.

jostle To push or shove roughly.  She JOSTLED her way through the crowd.

jujitsu Overall term for the Japanese art of unarmed self-defense, judo and karate being the most popular systems.

kung fu The Chinese version of jujitsu.

junction A joining point in a physical sense.  They met at the railroad JUNCTION.

juncture Also a joining, but more in the sense of a turning point.  Their marriage was at a critical JUNCTURE.

jungle Land dense and wet with tropical vegetation; a general reference for any hostile environment:  a JUNGLE of corruption.

rain forest Essentially the same as a jungle, but currently preferred by environmentalists:  Sting's world tour to save the RAIN FORESTS of Brazil.

○ While rain forest seems to be winning the usage war in the physical sense, jungle is here to stay for dangerous places in general: "The downtown area has become a jungle."

K

kin Short for kinfolk, or a person's relatives.

kith This encompasses friends as well as relatives.

○ Both kith and kin are plural words and endure as a duo largely with those who love alliteration.

kudos Praise and celebrity.
lucre Financial gain.

✎ ✎ Her book brought her critical KUDOS, but the sales did not add up to much LUCRE.

❂ Kudos is singular: "Kudos was given." However, this is gradually changing under user pressure, and it may soon be considered correct to say "Kudos were given.".

L

lactovegetarian Someone who does not eat meat, but does eat some animal products like milk and cheese.
vegan A strict vegetarian whose diet consists of grains, fruits, and vegetables.

languid Listless; lacking energy. ✎ She was LANGUID from the effects of a virus.
limpid Clear or unclouded, with no link to the word spelled by the first four letters. ✎ The crisp, blue sky matched her LIMPID blue eyes.

lay This is the verb to use with a direct object. ✎ Don't try to LAY the blame on me!
lie This is the verb to use in a sentence without a direct object. ✎ LIE down and take a nap.

left brain The part of the brain that controls the right side of the body and is linked with speech and calculating ability.
right brain The part of the brain that controls the left side of the body and is linked with spatial and artistic abilities.

legato Music with a smooth sound, without any noticeable interruption between the notes.

staccato Music that's disjointed rather than smooth.

legend Any story or person so much written and talked about that fact and fiction are no longer distinguishable.
myth A legendary story that currently embodies anything not to be accepted as a fact.
✎ ✎ A MYTH persists that rock 'n' roll LEGEND Elvis Presley is not really dead.

liable Having a probability arising from regular tendencies or past practices. ✎ Smokers are more LIABLE to have heart disease than nonsmokers.
likely A probability arising from unprecedented actions or behavior. ✎ Since he was a first-time offender, it's LIKELY that he'll receive a light sentence.

libel To publish damaging misinformation about someone. ✎ The publishers hired a top LIBEL lawyer to bulletproof their latest celebrity biography.
slander To say false and damaging things about someone. ✎ If you continue to SLANDER me in your public remarks, you'll hear from my lawyer!

libretto The text for a musical work, either original or adapted from a book or play. ✎ The LIBRETTOS for some of Mozart's most famous operas were written by Lorenzo da Ponte.
lyrics The words of a song. ✎ Andrew Lloyd Webber composed the music for *Phantom of the Opera*, but credit for the LYRICS belong to Charles Hart.

loath Unwilling. ✎ I'm LOATH to give up until I've explored every alternative.
loathe To detest. ✎ I LOATHE bigotry.

low fat Having less than 3 grams of fat per serving.
reduced fat Having no more than 50 percent of the fat content of the manufacturer's or industry's similar products.

✪ These definitions were formulated to make labels more consumer-friendly.

lugubrious Mournful or dismal.
salubrious Invigorating and refreshing.
   ✎ ✎ A week of working in the fresh mountain air had the SALUBRIOUS effect of replacing his LUGUBRIOUS expression with a big smile.

lumpectomy Breast cancer operation that involves the removal of the malignancy and some surrounding tissue and lymph nodes, but not the breast.
mastectomy Breast cancer operation involving the removal of the entire breast and often other tissue as well.

lunar eclipse This occurs two or three times a year, when the earth is between the sun and the moon and the shadow of the earth falls on the moon.
solar eclipse This occurs when the moon is between the earth and the sun, hiding the sun as the moon's shadow falls on the earth.

lunge To move forward suddenly in a disruptive or theatening manner. ✎ He LUNGED into our midst like a whirlwind on a summer day.
lurch To sway unsteadily or helplessly. ✎ Gathering her strength, she LURCHED toward him, then collapsed like a toppling wall.

luxuriant Growing abundantly: ✎ a LUXURIANT head of hair; ✎ a LUXURIANT garden.
luxurious Tending to extreme elegance and comfort: ✎ a LUXURIOUS lifestyle; ✎ LUXURIOUS surroundings.

Mafia The name most commonly associated with "organized crime"; also known as the Sicilian Mafia, for its origins, and "La Cosa Nostra," meaning "Our Thing."

Triad This Chinese counterpart of the Sicilian Mafia is one of the fastest-rising criminal organizations in the United States.

magnificent Very grand.

munificent Extremely generous.

✎ ✎ His MUNIFICENT gift helped to build a MAGNIFICENT addition to our library.

majority The number by which the votes cast for a winning candidate or issue exceeds all the remaining votes. ✎ Six of the ten members of board voted to fire the company president, four voted against it, which means he was ousted by a MAJORITY of two.

plurality In a multicandidate race, the number by which the votes cast for the winner exceeds those for the next-highest contender. ✎ Of the 1,800 votes cast, A got 1,000 votes, B got 500, and C got 300—a 500-vote PLURALITY.

○ When no specific numbers are involved, as in general reference to "the greater part or more than half," *majority* is usually the best choice. ✎ A MAJORITY of those in the audience were senior citizens.

maladroit Pertaining to bungling or clumsiness: ✎ The MALADROIT skater suffered many bruises.

malapropism A linguistic clumsiness wherein one word is confused for another, often with humorous results. ✎ I like your bat (instead of hat).

malady A disease or illness. ✎ He suffered from a serious but curable MALADY.

72

malaise An indefinite feeling of weakness or uneasiness.
✎ The news afflicted us with a hard-to-shake MALAISE.

mammal One of the thousands of vertebrate species, including humans, with self-regulating body temperature and hair or fur.
marsupial Any mammal (such as kangaroos or opossums) found in Australia, Central or South America, or, in the case of the possum, North America, whose females do not form placentas during pregnancy.

mammogram An X-ray examination of the breast to detect evidence of cancer.
sonogram An examination with an electronic instrument called an olliscope to detect abnormal tissue structures; often used in conjunction with mammography.
◐ See also *lumpectomy*.

mandible The lower jaw bone.
maxilla The upper jaw bone.

manifold Many and varied. ✎ The gorgeous and MANIFOLD colors of fall.
multiple Something with many parts or elements. ✎ We were offered MULTIPLE options.

marsh An open area of wetland covered by grasses and cattails.
swamp A wetland dominated by trees.

masochist Someone who relishes pain and humiliation.
sadist Someone who relishes inflicting pain and humiliation.
sadomasochist Someone who is both of the above.

mass-market paperback A small, softbound book for a large general audience, cheaper than a comparable hardbound book—but no longer cheap.

trade paperback A more expensive, more diversely sized paperback book for smaller, more specialized audiences.

masterful Outstanding, often with the added meaning of bossiness.
masterly Outstanding.
> ✎ ✎ He was a MASTERLY performer, but his off-stage manner was more modest than MASTERFUL.
> ○ Keep in mind that either word is okay to describe expertise, but only masterful carries the implication of superiority or bossiness.

meat loaf A mixture of chopped meat and various flavorings and binding ingredients (onion, ketchup, egg, bread crumbs, etc.), baked in a loaf pan and served hot or cold as a main dish.
paté A loaf-shaped spread made of fish or meats and generally served as an appetizer.
> ○ Some hosts slice their best meat loaf very thin and dish it up as a paté.

melody One musical note following another to produce a pattern; in popular songs, the element that sticks in your mind and makes you hum.
harmony Several musical tones played together; the musical support system for a melody.

mendacious Pertaining to untruthfulness or deceit. ✎ The stories told about him were MENDACIOUS.
veracious Pertaining to the truth. ✎ He was a VERACIOUS witness.
voracious Very hungry. ✎ He was a VORACIOUS reader.

mercurial Having rapid mood swings, especially upward; from the multiskilled Roman god Mercury. ✎ A MERCURIAL personality.
saturnine Gloomy and forbidding. ✎ A SATURNINE expression.

74

✪ See also chameleonic.

meretricious Based on pretense; insincere. ✎ The place has a certain MERETRICIOUS charm that strikes you as soon as you enter the glitzy lobby.
meritorious Actions that deserve praise or reward. ✎ A gold watch will never repay his many years of MERITO-RIOUS service.

metaphor The figurative use of a word to suggest a likeness to a dissimilar thing or idea. ✎ The sky was an artist's canvas. ✎ She was a whirlwind of activity.
simile A more direct comparison of two dissimilar things, introduced by like or as. ✎ She moved as swiftly as a bird on the wing.
✪ Both figures of speech are created and used by ordinary people as well as poets and writers. The best become part of the language mainstream.

meticulous Careful and attentive to every detail. ✎ She was METICULOUS about her work.
scrupulous Anything involving conscientiousness. ✎ She was SCRUPULOUS about doing her homework.

mildew A coating or discoloration that affects things exposed to moisture. ✎ The clothes she'd left in the beach house were ruined by MILDEW.
mold A fungus growth on food that indicates decay. ✎ The refrigerator was empty, save for some MOLDY cheese.

militate To influence strongly, more often than not in a negative sense. ✎ Tom's abrasive manner MILITATES against his forming lasting friendships.
mitigate To reduce in influence or severity; to moderate. ✎ His charm and good looks MITIGATED his untidy appearance. ✎ His youth was a MITIGATING factor.
✪ The against that often follows militate has no place after mitigate.

misanthrope An I-hate-everybody person, men as well as women.

misogamist A man who hates marriage.

misogynist A man who hates women.

modus operandi A method of working.

modus vivendi A truce before or instead of settling a dispute.

momentous Very important.

monumental Important, large and enduring, like a monument.

   ✎ ✎ It was a MOMENTOUS achievement that would have a MONUMENTAL effect on history.

monotheistic Believing in a single God.

polytheistic Believing in more than one god.

   ✪ Both words have Greek origins: theos for God, mono for single, and poly for many.

mouse A small rodent, $3\frac{1}{2}$ to 4 inches long with a 2- to 3-inch tail.

rat A rodent at least twice as long as a mouse and with a 5- to 8-inch long tail.

mousse A dessert of whipped cream mixed with sweetened ingredients and frozen without stirring; also fruits, meats or vegetables thickened with gelatin, or the nonedible mousses used to style hair.

parfait A frozen dessert of beaten egg whites (or yolks) cooked with hot syrup and combined with a mixture of ice cream, fruit, and whipped cream.

musical A show with music and dancing. The best modern musicals have a story line with the songs growing out of the story and not just an interlude. ✎ Oklahoma was the first Broadway MUSICAL to integrate music and story.

revue A musical show with songs and dancing but no story.

nadir Lowest point, borrowed from the astronomical term for the point in the celestial sphere precisely below the observer point.

zenith Highest point; from the astronomical high point in the celestial sphere, above the observer's head.

nauseate To cause physical or intellectual nausea.

nauseous Pertaining to that which induces nausea.

✎ ✎ The NAUSEOUS conditions in many homeless shelters are enough to NAUSEATE anyone.

nautical mile A measurement based on the circumference of the earth, which is divided into 360 degrees, with each degree divided into 60 minutes. ✎ The standard International Nautical mile equals 1,852 meters or 6,075.10333 feet.

knot The term used for nautical miles per hour: ✎ 1 knot = 1,852 meters per hour.

nefarious Wicked, to the extreme: ✎ a NEFARIOUS criminal; ✎ a NEFARIOUS scheme.

notorious Famous, usually in a negative way: ✎ a NOTORIOUS gambler; ✎ a NOTORIOUS show-off.

neurotic Of abnormal or excessive behavior without identifiable physical cause: ✎ NEUROTIC habits; ✎ NEUROTIC anxiety.

psychotic Behavior accompanied by impaired mental functions or withdrawal from reality. ✎ His bad temper worsened into PSYCHOTIC explosions during which he became physically violent.

nickname A name used in addition to or instead of one's real name, often coined by friends. ✎ Buffalo Bill was the NICKNAME of William Frederick Cody, a famous buffalo hunter and U.S. Army scout.

pseudonym A name assumed by a writer. Samuel Langhorne Clemens became famous under his PSEUDONYM, Mark Twain.

stage name Name by which professional performers are known: Madonna (Madonna Louise Ciccone); John Denver (Henry John Deutschendorf, Jr.).

notable Worthy of notice.
noticeable Easily noticed.
  He was quiet and hardly NOTICEABLE. Yet, he was the most NOTABLE guest there.

numismatist A collector of coins, tokens, or paper money.
philatelist A stamp collector.

nymphomaniac A women whose sexual urges are excessive or uncontrollable.
satyr A nymphomaniac's male counterpart.

O

obscene Indecent actions or language. When she tripped him and snatched back her jewelry, the robber uttered an OBSCENE curse.

pornographic Books, movies, songs, etc. containing sexually explicit language or images. Television has brought subjects once considered PORNOGRAPHIC into America's living rooms.

obfuscation That which is clouded and confusing, especially communications that are top-heavy with passive, cumbersome language. The truth was well hidden beneath a mountain of bureaucratic OBFUSCATION.

obtuseness Not sharp or pointed but dull. ✎ They were too OBTUSE to appreciate the play's wit.
✪ See also turbid.

obsequious Overly accommodating. ✎ They were OBSE-QUIOUS in their eagerness to please.

unctuous In a false, ingratiating manner. ✎ His UNC-TUOUS concern rang as true as canned applause.

octogenarian A person over 80 and under 90 years old. ✎ All of China's OCTOGENARIAN leaders seem to be feeling their age.

septuagenarian A person over 70 and under 80 years old. ✎ Advertisers have discovered the buying power of many of today's SEPTUAGENARIANS.

octopus An eight-tentacled, soft-bodied sea creature.

squid A sea creature with ten arms around its mouth.

off-Broadway Plays presented at small theaters away from the Broadway stages. Some move to Broadway when they become successful. ✎ The record-breaking musical A Chorus Line began its fifteen-year run at New York's OFF-BROADWAY Public Theater.

off-off Broadway Like off-Broadway shows, but in even smaller and less conveniently located theaters. ✎ The musical The Fantastiks recently celebrated its thirtieth birthday at its OFF-OFF BROADWAY home.

official Formally authorized; established. ✎ The OFFICIAL takeover announcement followed weeks of rumors.

officious Bossy or interfering. ✎ Her OFFICIOUS manner is a coverup for her ignorance.

on the contrary A denial of a claim or statement, followed by a statement of the facts. ✎ Hate you? ON THE CONTRARY, I adore you!

to the contrary Establishing that the facts are the opposite of what's claimed. ✎ Despite all their claims TO THE CONTRARY, the evidence proves their guilt.

oncology The study of tumors.
ontology The philosophical study of existence.

opera A musical drama for the theater: ✎ Aida.
oratorio A church composition for voices and orchestra: ✎ Handel's oratorios; ✎ pop singer Paul McCartney's Liverpool Oratorio.
popera A new word evolving from pop (popular) opera for modern musicals: ✎ *Les Miserables.*

ophthalmologist A medical doctor who treats eye problems.
optician A professional who makes and sells lenses and eyeglasses.
optometrist A professional who measures vision range and is licensed to prescribe glasses.

ordinance An authorized regulation. ✎ The city council passed a new ORDINANCE.
ordnance Military equipment. ✎ He was assigned to the ORDNANCE division.

oscillate Move back and forth regularly. ✎ His mood, like a pendulum, OSCILLATED between cheer and gloom.
undulate To move in smooth, rippling motions. ✎ The dancers UNDULATED smoothly across the stage.

overarch To hang over, in the sense of taking precedence and affecting all related situations; a term popular with the media but not yet in standard dictionaries. ✎ OVER-ARCHING the new challenges in the economic world order are the currently stalemated trade negotiations.
overreach To aim beyond what's realistic for a situation or one's ability, probably the source for overarch. ✎ Greed led them to OVERREACH and eventually fail.

oxymoron The pairing of two contradictory concepts, usually in two words: ✍ jumbo shrimp; ✍ military intelligence; ✍ mildly psychotic.

palindrome A word or phrase that reads the same forward and backward: ✍ sexes; ✍ sagas; ✍ radar; ✍ Madam, I'm Adam.

pleonasm A redundant expression: ✍ young child; ✍ dive down; ✍ dry desert; ✍ end result.

P

palatable Pleasingly acceptable to the palate or mind: ✍ a PALATABLE choice; ✍ a PALATABLE dinner.

savory Like palatable, but primarily relating to the senses and thus also piquant and zesty: ✍ a SAVORY sauce; ✍ a SAVORY mix.

palate The sense of taste; specifically, the roof of the mouth. ✍ They found the cuisine of the country pleasing to the PALATE.

palette The range of colors used by anyone working with colors or, specifically, a board for mixing paints. ✍ The new clothes focused on a fall PALETTE.

palaver Idle chatter that's designed to flatter or persuade. ✍ You don't fool me with your PALAVER!

prattle Idle, silly chatter. ✍ They PRATTLED on without saying anything memorable.

paltry Insignificant and trivial.

petty Insignificant, pertaining to quality and quantity, and to human characteristics as well as things.
✍ ✍ Only a truly PETTY person would have bothered to argue over such a PALTRY sum.

81

panda A bearlike mammal with wooly fur and distinctive black and white markings; also called giant panda.

koala A marsupial with dense grayish fur.

    ✺ Neither is a bear!

panorama A wide-ranging or constantly changing view. ✎ Our window opened on the whole PANORAMA of city life.

vista A far view seen through a narrow expanse, or a far-reaching intellectual view. ✎ His VISTAS were limited by his limited education.

paradigm An example or model for excellence in human behavior. ✎ He is a PARADIGM of grace under fire.

prototype An example or model to be copied or adapted. ✎ Levittown, the first inexpensive suburban development, served as a PROTOTYPE for many other housing developments.

paragon An excellent person: ✎ a PARAGON of virtue.

virtuoso Also an excellent person, but specifically relating to ability: ✎ a violin VIRTUOSO; ✎ an athletic VIRTUOSO.

parakeet A small parrot, usually with a tapering tail.

parrot A tropical bird whose ability to mimic human speech accounts for the word's use to describe any mindless imitation or imitator.

parole A prisoner's release from jail after serving a partial sentence, with probationary conditions.

probation Conditions imposed by a judge following a guilty plea or verdict—fines, community service, etc.

pedagogue An instructor, who may or not be pedantic. ✎ He was one of the college's most learned PEDAGOGUES.

pedant A stickler for formal learning or rules who may or may not be a teacher. ✎ A typical PEDANT, he clings to rules like a vine.

penultimate Next to the last. This is not a synonym for final nor should the "pen" be misread as super or extra. ✎
I found the PENULTIMATE scene of the play more moving than the final one.

quintessential The most essential or finest. ✎ She's the
QUINTESSENTIAL artist.

ultimate Final. ✎ That's our ULTIMATE goal.

people The correct word for referring to a very large
group of individuals. ✎ The room was packed with
PEOPLE.

persons The correct word for describing a small group of individuals. ✎ We were the only three PERSONS present.

peremptory Not to be argued with or refused. ✎ His
PEREMPTORY manner brooked no opposition.

preemptive Taking first place, by virtue of prior right or
opportunity. ✎ He won the movie rights to the best-
selling novel with a PREEMPTIVE bid.

perfidious Disloyal, treacherous. ✎ A PERFIDIOUS friend
is worse than no friend.

pernicious Having a harmful effect or influence. ✎ Even
a completely unfounded rumor can have a PERNICIOUS
effect on a politician's career.

peripatetic Moving from place to place. ✎ Paris is the
PERIPATETIC novelist's latest setting.

peripheral On the outside; unessential. ✎ She had a
strictly PERIPHERAL interest in sports.

perpetrate To carry out; often associated with a crime: ✎
to PERPETRATE a hoax.

perpetuate To preserve or prolong. ✎ Pop culture writers have helped to PERPETUATE the Beatles' legend.

perquisite A special advantage accompanying a job; perk,
for short.

83

requisite Something required or necessary.

   ✎ ✎ She had all the REQUISITES of power—a male secretary, an office with a view, and PERQUISITES that included a limousine.

perspicacious Having keen mental perception.
perspicuous Clearly presented; understandable.

   ✎ ✎ Many readers praised not only his PERSPICACIOUS observations but the PERSPICUOUS style that demystified what many had thought of as an esoteric subject.

   ✺ If there were a top ten of confusing word pairs, this one would surely make the list.

phenomena More than one rarity.
phenomenon A rare fact or circumstance.

philanderer A man who likes romance without commitment.
philistine Someone who scorns cultural interests.

   ✎ ✎ Stay away from him! He's got a well-deserved reputation as a PHILANDERER. Worse still, he's a PHILISTINE who hasn't been within a mile of a book or a museum in years.

photographic memory The ability to vividly recall images. ✎ At sixteen, Peter displayed a PHOTOGRAPHIC MEMORY for places he'd been taken to as a toddler.
total recall An excellent memory. ✎ His TOTAL RECALL was a big plus for scoring high on tests.

pick-off A baseball term for surprise play in which a base runner with a long lead is caught away from the base by a sudden throw from the pitcher or catcher.
pick-up A baseball term for a ball caught immediately after it strikes the ground.

pie A pastry crust with fillings, with or without a top crust.

Pie also has broader positive associations: ✎ sweet as or easy as PIE.

tart A single-portion pastry with fruit or jam, usually without a top crust. As an adjective that describes a sharp taste or remark, this may take its meaning from unsweetened fruits used for some tarts, or from tartar for a fierce person. ✎ A TART retort to a question.

✎ ✎ The meal began with a spinach PIE and ended with a fruit TART.

piercing Sharply or shrilly penetrating.

pointed Sharp, not so much in the sense of penetrating shrilly as that of pointing at very directly.

✎ ✎ His POINTED look PIERCED her indifference.

plebiscite A public opinion vote on a proposal for a new measure, program, or law. ✎ The PLEBISCITE showed that the townspeople wanted the old movie house preserved as a public landmark.

referendum Like a plebiscite, but on a measure that may already have been passed by a legislative body. ✎ A 1990 Arizona REFERENDUM upheld a decision to eliminate a previously celebrated official holiday.

plod To move heavily and deliberately, without joy; associated with dullness. ✎ The story PLODS along lifelessly.

slog To plod along physically or figuratively, with the added suggestion of difficulty. ✎ I found it about as easy to SLOG through that book as through a dense swamp.

pop Originally a term for smooth, easy-listening songs of the '40s but currently a catchall for all commercially successful popular music.

rap Combination of dancing, talking, and singing in rhyme that has evolved from West African villages and '40s jazz to today's pop-spiced rap.

rock A very broad classification of diverse modern musical styles from early rock 'n' roll to folk rock, soft rock, hard rock, and rap 'n' rock.

○ See also *gospel.*

precipitate To cause (verb); abrubt (adjective). ✎ PRE-CIPITATE a disaster; ✎ a PRECIPITATE departure.

precipitous Pertaining to a steep incline: ✎ a PRECIPI-TOUS descent.

presage To indicate bad luck or events. ✎ For the super-stitious a black cat PRESAGES bad luck.

prophesy To predict things to come. ✎ No one seemed able to PROPHESY the recession's end.

prescribe To order or suggest that something be done. ✎ He PRESCRIBED a daily exercise program.

proscribe To disallow. ✎ A vegetarian diet PROSCRIBES the consumption of meat.

priggish Prim and self-righteous.

prim Excessively formal and proper.

✎ ✎ The PRIM manner that he once found charming seemed unpleasantly PRIGGISH with time.

principal Chief or main idea, person or persons. ✎ The PRINCIPAL shareholders voted him out. ✎ Scratch the surface of a good school and you're almost certain to find a good PRINCIPAL leading the way.

principle A guiding belief or theory. ✎ Why won't I do it? It's a matter of PRINCIPLE.

○ Principal can serve as a noun or adjective, but princi-ple is strictly a noun.

probity Pertaining to uprightness and honesty. ✎ He lacked the PROBITY expected of someone in his position.

propriety Conformity to appropriate standards. ✎ She was the very model of PROPRIETY.

prodigal Lavish or extravagant in behavior or person. ✎

They were PRODIGAL spenders.

prodigious Marvelous, amazing. ✎ In October trees shed their leaves at a PRODIGIOUS rate.

✎ ✎ John Updike's output of stories, essays, novels, and an autobiography, attest to his PRODIGIOUS energy and his PRODIGAL talents.

progesterone A female hormone, currently administered in combination with estrogen to prevent vaginal dryness, heart disease, and osteoporosis in women no longer producing their own hormones.

testosterone A male sex hormone produced in the testes which controls secondary sex characteristics.

prosody The study of metrical form and verse. ✎ The young poet could have benefited from a remedial course in PROSODY.

syntax The branch of grammar that deals with how words and sentences are put together. ✎ Kate was adept at spotting errors of SYNTAX in her sister's paper.

prostate A gland near the male bladder.

prostrate Cast down or a dejected state.

✎ ✎ He refused to let his PROSTATE operation PROSTRATE him.

prudent Wise behavior based on caution and foresight; the avoidance of rashness. ✎ It's PRUDENT to find another job before quitting the one you have.

sage Knowledgeable, astute, based on established wisdom. ✎ A book of quotations offers much SAGE advice of men and women from past and present times.

psychiatrist A physician who treats mental disorders.

clinical psychologist A nonmedical professional, generally with a doctoral degree, who treats people with mental problems.

psychotherapist A (usually nonmedical) professional who uses psychotherapy to help people to understand and resolve their mental and emotional problems.

pugnacious Apt to fight.
pusillanimous Cowardly.
    ✎ ✎ He was tough but not PUGNACIOUS, cautious but not PUSILLANIMOUS.

purvey To supply with. ✎ They PURVEY goods and services.
purview The scope of one's operations or view. ✎ The PURVIEW of their study was international.

Q

quagmire Wet, marshy ground that tends to give way under one's feet; more generally, any difficult situation. ✎ His financial empire was in a QUAGMIRE of debt.
quicksand A deep mass of loose sand and water which can swallow up unwary persons or animals; generally, anything hard to control. ✎ They were swept into a QUICKSAND of emotion.

quake To tremble from physical or emotional shock. ✎ His voice QUAKED with nervousness.
quiver A slight, nervous movement. ✎ As he entered, a QUIVER of excitement went through the crowd.

qualitative Concerned with quality. ✎ From a QUALITATIVE point of view, the meal was   so-so.
quantitative Concerned with quantities. ✎ From a QUANTITATIVE point of view, it was a good buy.

88

quarrelsome Pertaining to someone who tends to get into arguments easily.  He tends to be QUARRELSOME, especially about small points.

querulous Pertaining to someone who complains a lot.  They're QUERULOUS, hard-to-please people.

queasy Sick or uneasy.  I'm QUEASY about dealing with such a disreputable person.

squeamish Like queasy but with the additional meaning of over-fastidiousness or prudishness.  His SQUEAMISH attitude has no place in the operating room.

quell To overpower or suppress.  The president tried to QUELL the commotion about interpreting the new law.

quench To put an end to by satisfying.  He QUENCHED his thirst with a tall glass of iced tea.

quixotic Romantic but unrealistic and impractical.  His charmingly QUIXOTIC book had a very limited appeal.

sporadic Occurring intermittently, not on a regular basis.  Alas, our trysts have become quite SPORADIC.

quorum The number required for a group to hold a meeting.

quota A set amount to be done or given access to.

R

ramble To wander without a fixed aim:  to RAMBLE around town;  to RAMBLE from one subject to another.

range Like ramble, but suggesting a wide radius and not necessarily without a fixed purpose.  The book RANGES over many social problems and concludes with a chapter of suggestions for solving them.

89

rare Infrequent occurence or object.

scarce In short supply.

✎ ✎ With even necessities SCARCE, you can imagine how RARE luxuries are.

ratify To officially approve. ✎ Your signature will RATIFY our agreement.

sanction To not only approve but encourage enforcement.

✎ The writer urges us to enjoy ourselves more fully than our Puritan heritage SANCTIONS.

✪ In international law, sanctions represent approval of penalties against noncompliant states.

rebuff To snub or beat back. ✎ She REBUFFED his overtures of friendship.

rebut To prove someone wrong; to refute. ✎ He failed to REBUT their accusation.

redolent Suggestive or reminiscent of, as a fragrance or memory. ✎ The style she favored was REDOLENT of an earlier epoch.

redundant Excessively or unnecessarily repetitious. ✎ His constant and REDUNDANT reminders annoyed everyone.

referee One who arbitrates legal or other disputes.

umpire One who rules on plays in various sports, particularly baseball.

restful Providing rest or relaxation.

restive To be restless or uneasy.

✎ ✎ I enjoyed the RESTFUL weekend but to be there for a long time would make me RESTIVE.

reticent Disinclined to talk about one's thoughts.

taciturn Inclined to silence; uncommunicative and stern in manner.

✎ ✎ She was not a TACITURN person though she tended to be RETICENT about intimate matters.

rigorous Pertaining to strictness or severity.
vigorous Full of energy.
✎ ✎ Our company prides itself in maintaining RIGOR-OUS standards and a bright, VIGOROUS staff.

rite The entire ceremony associated with a special event or period.
ritual An activity associated with the rite.
✎ ✎ Kissing the bride is a RITUAL that's part of most wedding RITES.

rogue A dishonest person, generally more mischievous than evil: ✎ a charming ROGUE.
villain An evil, bad person: ✎ a murderous VILLAIN.

S

SAE Abbreviation for self-addressed envelope.
SASE Abbreviation for self-addressed, stamped envelope.
✎ ✎ Anyone who offers to mail information, will save time and money asking for a SAE, or better still, a SASE. To avoid confusion, spell it out and specify #10 (letter) or 9 x 12 (manuscript) size.

sampler A musical computer into which sounds are entered and converted into bits of digital information that can be played back any time.
synthethizer A device that creates its own sounds, which can then be changed electronically.
⟳ Some samplers store and create sounds.

sangfroid Cool and self-possessed behavior. _✎_ She greeted them with the SANGFROID of a queen.

savoir faire Social know-how and sophistication. _✎_ Our guide's charm and SAVOIR FAIRE made our visit especially memorable.

  ○ Two French conversational "seasoners."

sanguine Cheerfully confident. _✎_ Such a SANGUINE person would do well as a salesman.

tranquil Of a calm, undisturbed temperament or setting. _✎_ Sailboats moved gently across the TRANQUIL water.

scam Something fraudulent. _✎_ Many a get-rich-quick offer is a SCAM.

sham Something false or insincere. _✎_ His sincere manner was a SHAM.

schlemiel A Yiddish word for a misfit or fool.

schlimazl A Yiddish word for someone who seems chronically unlucky.

  _✎ ✎_ It takes a SCHLIMAZL in a hurry to hail a taxi driven by a SCHLEMIEL.

  ○ See also Hebrew.

scintillating Sparkling, as with talent, wit or enthusiasm: _✎_ a SCINTILLATING performance.

titillating From its literal meaning of tickling, this has come to mean anything that stimulates, usually with a sexual connotation: _✎_ a TITILLATING account of an event.

scrumptious Enjoyable, delicious.

sumptuous Expensive and luxurious.

  _✎ ✎_ Something can be scrumptious without being sumptuous or sumptuous without being scrumptious; for example, a SCRUMPTIOUS meal eaten in less than SUMPTUOUS surroundings.

  ○ Even those who never confuse the meaning sometimes stumble over the uous/ious endings.

seasonable Suitable to a season; timely. ✎ The invitation came at a SEASONABLE time.

seasonal Affected by the seasons. ✎ They could not keep up their mortgage with only SEASONAL job income.

self-publishing The process whereby authors act as publishers of their own work. This may include hiring others to print, bind, and distribute it.

vanity publishing Process whereby authors pay a publisher to print and distribute a book, instead of the other way around.

○ The first practice is a legitimate option; for the other, check out caveat emptor (see caveat).

sensual Pertaining to bodily pleasure, like food and sex. ✎ His manner was remarkably prim for one with such a SENSUAL face and body.

sensuous Pertaining to the aesthetic gratification of the senses. ✎ As we entered the apartment, we were immediately struck by the SENSUOUS fabrics and colors of its decor.

sinuous Pertaining to anything with many curves and bends. ✎ It is a SINUOUSLY unraveling tale about a woman's secret.

shareware Computer software for which users pay only after they try it out and become registered users. Users are encouraged to share their copies with other potential user-buyers.

software Programs (commercial, shareware or public domain) that instruct the machine (the hardware) how to perform its tasks, such as word processing.

vaporware Software that's announced but doesn't materialize.

shun To avoid or keep away from. ✎ "To SHUN him like the plague" was first used by Charles Dickens.

spurn To reject with disdain. ✎ She SPURNED me as if I were a worm.

signal When used as an adjective, signal refers to something unusual or important, likely to evoke immediate notice and response.

significant Of great importance.

    ✎ ✎ The new legislation is a SIGNAL achievement that will have a SIGNIFICANT effect on employees everywhere.

sledgehammer A long, heavy hammer often wielded with both hands; figuratively speaking, heavy-handedness: ✎ a SLEDGEHAMMER approach.

triphammer Another heavy hammer, but power-operated and therefore anything powerful: ✎ to work with TRIPHAMMER efficiency.

slink To move in a stealthy, guilty manner. ✎ I watched him SLINK away like a burglar.

slither To move with an unsteady slide. ✎ We SLITHERED across the icy road.

sludge Thick greasy mud, or anything with that appearance or feel.

slush Partly melted snow on the ground.

solar flares Sudden, tremendous outbursts of energy on the sun that send out strong X-rays and ultraviolet light. A strong flare sends out electrically charged atoms.

sunspots Less-bright regions on the surface of the sun, from tiny to large enough to swallow the whole earth.

solid Substantial or upstanding. ✎ She may seem flighty, but she's a SOLID and dedicated worker.

stolid Impassive, said of one who shows little emotion and is often considered to be dull: ✎ He seems rather STOLID for a rock star.

sonic boom A noise caused by the shock wave from an aircraft or other object traveling in the atmosphere at or above the speed of sound.

sonic speed The speed at which sound travels, approximately 760 miles per hour at sea level when the atmosphere is at standard conditions.

sophomoric Pretentious, know-it-all, like the behavior of some second-year students.

soporific Sleep-inducing, either by means of a drug or a boring situation.

✎ ✎ Their SOPHOMORIC antics had a SOPORIFIC effect on the audience.

specious Seemingly good but unable to hold up under closer scrutiny. ✎ His argument was so persuasive that no one questioned the SPECIOUS reasoning behind it.

spurious False, inauthentic. ✎ He gave SPURIOUS evidence.

spire A tall pointed structure that often caps a steeple.

steeple A tower on top of a building.

sprint To run at top speed, usually for a short distance.

spurt A sudden burst or effort.

✎ ✎ Mustering a final SPURT of energy, he SPRINTED to the goal line.

squall A sudden, violent windstorm, with or without rain or snow.

tempest A long-lasting violent windstorm, with or without rain or snow.

❍ Both storms are often used figuratively: ✎ The scandal quickly changed from a SQUALL to a TEMPEST.

squeak A short, high-pitched cry or sound; also an informal verb for a narrow escape. ✎ She managed to SQUEAK by with a passing grade.

squeal A long, shrill cry or sound; also a slang term for what you do when you become an informant. ✎ He

95

gave a SQUEAL of terror when they threatened to beat him up for SQUEALING to the police.

stalactite Icicle-shaped mineral deposit developed from the water drippings on the roof of a cave.

stalagmite Like a stalactite but pointing up from the cave floor.

    ✎ ✎ The constantly dripping STALACTITES caused many STALAGMITES to form on the cave's floor.

stanza Lines that form a section of a poem or song. ✎ I can remember only the first STANZA from that song.

verse A single line of a poem or song. ✎ "To be or not to be: that is the question" is one of Shakespeare's best-known VERSES.

stationary Fixed or inert. ✎ I pedal three miles to nowhere on my daily STATIONARY bike ride.

stationery Writing materials. ✎ Her collages often included bits of colorful STATIONERY.

strategy An overall plan of procedure.

tactic The means for putting the plan into action.

    ✎ ✎ Our STRATEGY for attacking the problem required strong, but not strong-arm, TACTICS.

    ○ Both terms, though military in origin, are very much in the mainstream of everyday English.

stultify To make ineffective; to frustrate. ✎ His refusal to talk to us STULTIFIED the investigation.

stupefy To stun or dull the mind. ✎ We were STUPEFIED by the heat and lack of stimulation.

stump To puzzle: ✎ to be STUMPED for an answer.

stymie Block progress: ✎ a strike that STYMIES production.

supersonic Faster than the speed of sound.

ultrasonic Of frequencies above those that affect the human ear (more than 20,000 vibrations per second).

surge A forward rush, like a wave. ✎ She was overcome by a sudden SURGE of anger.

zoom To move quickly, often with a buzzing sound. ✎ The cyclists ZOOMED past us.

T

tangelo A hybrid between the grapefruit and the tangerine.

tangerine Another fruit of the citrus family, colored a deep-orange and with easily peeled skin; also known as a mandarin orange.

○ Many people expect tangelos to have a deeper color because they're unaware of their link to the paler grapefruit.

tanker A sea giant that hauls oil and other liquids around the world. Some tankers are 1,300 feet long and 200 feet wide.

tugboat A small but powerful and sturdy boat that guides large ships in and out of the harbor.

tarantella A lively Italian dance once thought to be a remedy for the bite of a tarantula.

tarantula A type of tropical spider capable of inflicting painful but not lethal bites.

tasteful In good taste, appealing.

tasty Having a good flavor.

✎ ✎ Even though the restaurant's decor was not very TASTEFUL, the meal was very TASTY.

temerity Reckless boldness.

timidity Excessive fearfulness.

✎ ✎ One big win often turns a TIMID investor into one with too much TEMERITY.

temporal Pertaining to a short time; also to world affairs. ✎ The diplomat and his son were preoccupied with their own TEMPORAL concerns—the father with international peace, the son with racing cars.

temporizing Pertaining to evasiveness in order to gain time. ✎ His TEMPORIZING answer told nothing.

that Relative pronoun used to introduce statements essential to the meaning of a sentence.

which Relative pronoun used to introduce statements that describe or explain without being essential. ✎ ✎ My book was the first work by an unknown THAT they ever published, WHICH was fortunate for me.

thunderbolt One burst of lightning accompanying thunder and, by extension, any shock. ✎ The news hit me like a THUNDERBOLT.

thunderclap The sound of thunder and, by extension, any very loud noise. ✎ Their cheers rang through the hall like THUNDERCLAPS.

toil Strenuous or prolonged work.

travail Painful or difficult effort. ✎ ✎ After much TOIL and TRAVAIL she gave birth to triplets.

tortuous Twisting, winding, or crooked roads or waterways, and, by implication, anything twisted or deceitful.

torturous Excruciatingly painful or uncomfortable. ✎ ✎ He suffered TORTUROUS consequences from the TORTUOUS web he wove.

town Smaller than a city and larger than a village, a town includes residential, commercial and public buildings. It has its own fixed boundaries and some governmental powers and can be a suburb of a city.

village Smaller than a town and often a neighborhood within a larger municipality.

✎ ✎ He commuted from the VILLAGE of Thomaston, in the suburban TOWN of Great Neck, to his job in nearby New York City.

✪ The word town is used to refer to the main shopping area of either a town or city.

✪ See also edge city.

trammel To confine or hinder. ✎ I felt TRAMMELED by responsibility.

trample To crush with the feet or treat harshly. ✎ She TRAMPLED on my feelings like leaves on the ground.

transient Short-term. ✎ Her pain was TRANSIENT.

transitional Pertaining to a form or period of change. ✎ The TRANSITIONAL stage between adolescence and adulthood can be difficult.

translucent Permitting light to pass through, but not transparent: ✎ a TRANSLUCENT frosted glass door.

transparent Capable of being seen through: ✎ TRANS-PARENT curtains; ✎ a TRANSPARENT excuse.

transsexual One who identifies with the opposite sex, sometimes undergoing a sex change operation.

transvestite One who has a strong urge to wear the clothes of the opposite sex.

triumphal Pertaining to the celebration of a triumphant event or person.

triumphant Jubilant; victorious.

✎ ✎ The TRIUMPHANT hero returned to his home town for a TRIUMPHAL celebration.

tumultuous Noisy and disorderly: ✎ a TUMULTUOUS crowd.

turbulent Violently agitated, disturbed, or confused: ✎ TURBULENT times; ✎ a TURBULENT sea.

turbid Cloudy or muddy and thus unclear.
turgid Swelled up, like a river or pompous language.
　🖎 🖎 "Bureaucratese" with its TURBID sentence structure and TURGID vocabulary seems designed to confuse rather than enlighten.
　❍ See also obfuscation.

UHF Acronym for ultra-high frequency—the range of the electromagnetic spectrum used for TV stations with channels numbered from 14 through 83.
VHF Acronym for very high frequency—the range of electromagnetic frequencies used by TV stations numbered from 2 through 13.

uncanny Extremely puzzling and a source of wonder.
unearthly Strange enough to suggest being out of this world.
　🖎 🖎 He had an UNCANNY talent to make his often UNEARTHLY tales real and believable, even for readers who usually prefer more earthbound fare.

ureter The tubes leading from the kidney to the bladder.
urethra The channel through which urine leaves the body.

vacillate To go back and forth like a pendulum; to be unable to act decisively.
waver To show uncertainty or weaken.

✎ ✎ They VACILLATED for months before making a decision. However, they were so torn between their idealism and fear that they soon WAVERED again.

vapid Dull, uninteresting; something gone flat. ✎ a VAPID facial expression; ✎ VAPID conversation.

vaporous Characteristic of the diffused moisture causing fog and thus anything vaguely formed or unsubstantial. ✎ An unrealistic, VAPOROUS theory.

venal Pertaining to wrongdoing, identified with corruption. ✎ His administration was rife with VENAL practices.

venial Minor, forgivable. ✎ Her repeated lateness is an annoying but VENIAL sin.

vilify To defame: ✎ Press reports that VILIFY.

vivify To give or bring to life: ✎ a biography that VIVIFIES a historic personage.

viola Instrument that looks like an overgrown violin, but with thicker strings that produce a distinctly deeper and more mellow sound. ✎ The VIOLA is mostly a team player, rarely a soloist.

violin The smallest of the common string instruments. ✎ Because the VIOLIN has so many shades of expressions, composers often entrust it with their most beautiful ideas and solo parts.

○ Violins and violas are played with their heads resting against the players' chins. The larger string instruments, the cello and the double bass, are propped up on metal spikes.

vouchsafe To grant, in a condescending manner or as a favor.

vow To earnestly promise or pledge.

✎ ✎ The only time she saw him VOUCHSAFE a smile was when she VOWED she would never speak to him again.

wane To show decreasing enthusiasm or strength.
wax To show increasing enthusiasm or strength.

✎ ✎ Political imperialism is on the WANE. At the same time economic unionism is WAXING.

✎ ✎ As use of this word pair has WANED, confusion about which means what has WAXED.

✪ Our first example, from a column by word maven William Safire, may be an indication that reports of the death of wax and wane are premature.

wangle To accomplish by cleverness, contrivance. ✎ He managed to WANGLE a free ticket for himself.
wrangle An angry argument or to argue angrily. ✎ Let's not get into a WRANGLE over this!

warp The lengthwise threads of a woven fabric.
weft The horizontal threads of a woven fabric.

✪ In more general usage, these terms are paired to describe any underlying structure: ✎ ✎ the WARP and WEFT on which an institution is built.

wary Cautious, suspicious behavior.
wily Ruled by cunning.

✎ ✎ I'm WARY of doing business with such a WILY individual.

water repellent Truth-in-advertising has replaced claims for 100 percent waterproof with this term for products that resist water penetration.
watertight Made to prevent water from getting in; when used in a broader sense, anything impossible to disprove. ✎ He had a WATERTIGHT alibi.

whim A fanciful, often irrational, idea or action. ✎ He quit his job on a WHIM.

whimsy A fanciful and often playful idea. ✎ The masks worn by the guests lent a touch of WHIMSY to the festivities.

○ Whim is always a noun, but whimsical is an accepted and popular adjective form of whimsy.

whirligig Any spinning toy or a person who continuously whirls about: ✎ she's a WHIRLIGIG of activity.

whirlybird Slang alternative to chopper for helicopter: ✎ to report on traffic from a WHIRLYBIRD.

who's Contraction for who is or who has. ✎ WHO'S calling?

whose Possessive form for of whom or of which. ✎ WHOSE life is it anyway?

wine Fermented juice from fruits or plants.

spirits An umbrella term for all alcoholic drinks, from hard liquor to wines.

✎ ✎ Their WINE and SPIRITS store specialized in fine imported WINES.

wizened Shriveled, as an aged person's face. ✎ His WIZENED face seemed to radiate contentment.

wrinkled A smooth surface with ridges or creases: ✎ Her clothes were WRINKLED and dishevelled.

✎ ✎ The years had etched a mass of WRINKLES into her WIZENED face.

○ You can have wrinkles without looking wizened.

x-chromosome Sex chromosome of which females have two and males one.

y-chromosome Sex chromosome of which males have one and females none.

xebec A three-masted sailing ship with a long overhanging bow and stern. Pronounced "zee-beck."

yawl A type of sailboat; also a ship's small boat.

yang The masculine, active, or positive and assertive principle associated with light.

yin The feminine, passive principle associated with darkness.

○ These terms from Chinese philosophy are usually used together to show a complementary relationship.

zap From its original meaning of destroying with gunfire, this now applies to ending an activity or action.

zip A noun for energy and liveliness and, informally, to act or move fast or energetically.

✎ ✎ When you tape a television show, you can ZAP all the commercials and thus ZIP through in a fraction of the time you'd spend watching it live.

zealous enthusiastic or devoted to the point of excess. ✎ She felt smothered by his ZEALOUS devotion.

zestful Pertaining to keen, wholehearted enjoyment or interest. ✎ The play's shortcomings were offset by the ZESTFUL performances of the actors.

Rhymed Review

Like any verses, these will probably prove more helpful and enjoyable nibbled a few bites at a time than gulped down at one sitting. The rhymes are arranged to match the organization of the text, from A-word to Y-word entries. Each draws on one or more words from a single entry of grouped definitions in one of the following four formats:

Fill-In Rhymes
The dashes between the first and last letter(s) equal the number of letters to be filled in. Capsule definitions to help with the fill-ins appear nearby most.

"Choice" Words
The rhyme is followed by the word choices to fit the blanks. You choose which goes where.

"Choice" Definitions
The rhymes are followed by several featured words and correct and incorrect definitions. You choose the correct one.

Riddle Rhymes
These question and answer rhymes are just for enjoyment: there's nothing to fill in.

1. When a king named Rob
   a - - - - - - - d his job   *(a) formally resigned*
   His royal rights he did a - - - - - - e.   *(b) do away with*
   But his cousin Prince Sean
   Quickly seized the crown
   And to himself royal power did a - - - - - - e.   *(c) seized hold of*

2. To her a - - - - - tion   *(a) charge*
   "You're having an affair!"
   He r - - - - - - - - - ed: *(b) counter-charged*
   "You treat me like air!"

3. His c - - - - - c procrastination   *(a) persistent*
   caused her a - - - e exasperation   *(b) intense*

4. It's hard to (a) _____ changes
   to cure many social ills
   When they (b) _____ the voters'
   income tax bills.   *affect or effect?*

5. An (a) _____ asked to believe in a deity
   declares: "Only if you show me!"
   Ask an (b) _____ to believe and pray
   And he'll unhesitatingly say, "No way!"
          agnostic or atheist?

---

5. (a)agnostic, (b) atheist
4. (a) effect, (b) affect
3. (a) chronic, (b) acute
2. (a) accusation, (b) recriminated
1. (a) abdicated, (b) abrogate, (c) arrogate

108

6. Instead of working every day,
   I'd like on a - - - - - - - e days to play.   *(a) not every day*
   But my boss feels rather negative
   about my every-other-day a - - - - - - - - - e.   *(b) choice*
                                                            between

7. Three girls from Tennessee
   Were very popular (a) _____.
   When (b) _____ Alison tied the knot
   With (c) _____ Allan from Hottentot,
   Friends and (d) _____ from every coast
   Came to the wedding their union to toast.
                       alumnae, alumna, alumnus or alumni?

8. When Dennis met Alice
   She was a tennis n - - - - e.   *(a) beginner*
   Though she still maintains
       her a - - - - - r pose,   *(b) nonprofessional*
   She's now good enough to serve to the pros.

9. He was an a - - - - - - e date   *(a) agreeable*
   But, alas, an i - - - - - - l mate.   *(b) disagreeable*

10. Eager Ed urged, "Come on, let's go!"
    Anxious Annie said, "Take it slow."
    She fretted about what might occur
    A happy ending to deter.
                       EAGER: *(a) keen, (b) enterprising*
                       ANXIOUS: *(a) very scared, (b) somewhat uneasy*

---

10. eager (a), anxious (b)
9. (a) amicable, (b) inimical
8. (a) novice, (b) amateur
7. (a) alumnae, (b) alumna, (c) alumnus, (d) alumni
6. (a) alternate, (b) alternative

11. Whether you readily (a) _____
    Or after due deliberation (b) _____ ,
    You must proceed
    As you agreed.   *assented or consented?*

12. Rest a - - - - - d   *(a) secure*
    My house is i - - - - - d.   *(b) financially safeguarded*
    So, if into my well you fall,
    My insurance company I will call
    To pay the bill
    For your spill.

13. He was a - - - - - - - ed to be admonished,   *(a) surprised*
    A - - - - - - ed to have his car impounded.   *(b) stunned*
    And with his troubles thus compounded,
    He was simply d - - - - - - ded.   *(c) speechless*

14. Her _____ expression
    Echoed my depression.   *baleful or doleful?*

15. When they think stock prices
    Will go low, not high
    The (a) _____ will sell
    And the (b) _____ will buy.   *bears or bulls?*

---

15. (a) bears, (b) bulls
14. doleful
13. (a) astonished, (b) astounded, (c) dumbfounded
12. (a) assured, (b) insured
11. (a) assented, (b) consent

16. When a woody plant would fit in a tub
    What you've got is a s - - - b.   *(a) smaller than a tree*
    What if it's shorter still?
    Call it a b - - h, if you will.   *(b) very small woody plant*
    Clever gardeners combine both with trees
    Into a collection of s - - - - - - - ies. *(c) area of mixed plants*

17. A b - - - - - - ly in my garden   *(a) flying creature*
    is a treasured guest.
    But a m - - h in my closet   *(b) it flies by night*
    Is an unwelcome pest.

18. A c - - - - n's a valley that's narrow and deep
                    (a) usually has a river running through
    Call it a g - - - e if it's also quite steep.
                    (b) may also have a river, just steeper
    If you're looking for a valley
    Where you and your pals can dally,
    Then a g - - n   *(c) narrow valley*
    or a d - - l   *(d) small wooded valley*
    Will be right up your alley.

19. One's (a) _____ can vanish like soup du jour
    But good (b) _____ will forever endure.
                    character or reputation?

19. (a) reputation, (b) character
18. (a) canyon, (b) gorge, (c) glen, (d) dell
17. (a) butterfly, (b) moth
16. (a) shrub, (b) bush, (c) shrubberies

111

20. Concertos and sonatas display
    A virtuoso's instrumental forte.
    Symphonies on the other hand
    Star every musician in the band.

    CONCERTO: *(a) music for piano, (b) music for the flute*
    (c) music for any one instrument and an orchestra
    SONATA: *(a) music for an orchestra and an instrument,*
    (b) music for the piano, (c) music for any instrument

21. When you use valves to
    Switch from high sounds to low
    It's a (a) _____ or its shorter cousin,
    The (b) _____ , that you blow.   *trumpet or cornet?*

22. The audience applause
    rang through the hall
    So all the singers
    Took a c - - - - - n c - - l.   *(a) took another bow*
    The fans' insistent cries
    Of "Bravo" and "More"
    Induced the prima donna
    To sing an e - - - - e.   *(b) extra song*

23. For our c - - - - - - - y outing   *(a) regularly scheduled*
    To paint the town
    Gloomy Gus casts off
    His h - - - - - - l frown.   *(b) tending to unconscious*
                                            regularity

23. (a) customary, (b) habitual
22. (a) curtain call, (b) encore
21. (a) trumpet, (b) cornet
20. concerto (c), sonata (c)

112

24. For political favors he had done
    A cushy s - - - - - - e he won. *(a) a job with more*
    perks than work
    But when he became the c - - - - - - e *(b) center of attention*
    Of the Press's patronage exposure
    Alas, his cushy job was soon undone.

25. People with no literary bent in particular
    Often talk in a unique sort of v - - - - - - - - r. *(a) regional*
    expressions
    Others in their speech reflect
    Their place of origin's d - - - - - t. *(b) special language*
    of a region
    J - - - - n's a special language too. *(c) trade or sports talk*
    It's linked to what you do.

26. Your service is
    - - - - - - - - - ly inefficient *extremely bad*
    And in civility deficient.

27. I've made my disdain quite plain
    Without deigning to explain
    Why I'd rather have less
    Than accept his largess.
    DISDAIN: *(a) hatred, (b) dissatisfaction, (c) scorn*
    DEIGN: *(a) try, (b) condescend, (c) take time*

28. On my low-cal diet I often dream
    That I'm subsisting in a d - - - - t *(a) arid land*
    On d - - - - - ts topped with cream. *(b) last course of a meal*

---

28. (a) desert, (b) dessert
27. deign (b), disdain (c)
26. egregious
25. (a) vernacular, (b) dialect, (c) jargon
24. (a) sinecure, (b) cynosure

113

29. QUESTION: If for space you're not terribly pressed,
What alternatives for e.g. and i.e. would work best?

ANSWER: "For example" will work fine instead of e.g. and
"that is" makes plain English out of the Latin i.e.

30. (a)Envy is just an emotional wart
But (b)jealousy can tear you apart.
ENVY: *(a) disdain, (b) covet*
JEALOUSY: *(a) desire, (b) begrudge*

31. A trip to a place far away and e - - - - c   *(a) different*
Can make you feel free and enormously e - - - - c. *(b) sexual*

32. If you (a) _____
What you gain
When you (b) _____ a rule,
Man, you're a fool.   *flaunt or flout?*

33. This f - - - - - o of word definitions   *medley*
Aims at boosting your precision.

34. If you run any _____ ,
You'll be ahead of Arthur.   *farther or further?*

---

34. farther
33. farrago
32. (a) flaunt, (b) flout
31. (a) exotic, (b) erotic
30. envy (b), jealousy (b)

114

35. A _____ couple from Maryland
Had enough kids for a marching band.   *fecund or feckless?*

36. As I _____ and fly
Like a kite through the sky
I never stop hoping
that I'll keep coping.   *founder or flounder?*

37. Curious George s - - - es.   *(a) looks intently*
Angry Andy g - - - es.   *(b) looks angry*
And lascivious Larry l - - rs   *(c) looks slyly*
When a risque remark he hears.

38. When George the g - - - - - t   *(a) fine food lover*
Dishes ups a buffet
It's guaranteed to be
Gastronomically okay.

You'll enjoy a meal
with g - - - - - - d Camille   *(b) quantity food lover*
If you're in the mood
For tons of food.

39. It was a murder (a) _____ and weird
Committed by a man with a (b) _____ beard.
    grisly or grizzly?

35. fecund
36. flounder
37. (a) stares, (b) glares, (c) leers
38. (a) gourmet, (b) gourmand
39. (a) grisly, (b) grizzly

115

40. To enjoy _____ with apple sauce
    You don't have to be Jewish because
    They're delicious and even nutritious.

    latkes or hamentaschen?

41. If a popular lecturer you want to entice,
    A small _____ may not suffice.

    stipend or honorarium

42. It's hard to believe
    That anything so h - - - - - dous   *(a) awful*
    Could be produced by one
    With an IQ so s - - - - - dous.   *(b) great*

43. The _____ does not bewail
    a life filled with travail.   *hedonist or stoic?*

44. I (a) _____ from what she said
    That her love affair is dead.
    But in no way did she (b) _____
    That she won't try again
    With another guy.   *infer or imply?*

45. (a) I - - - - - - y exempts you from disease or duty.
    A crime without time best describes (b) i - - - - - - y.

    immunity or impunity?

---

45. (a) immunity, (b) impunity
44. (a) infer, (b) imply
43. stoic
42. (a) horrendous, (b) stupendous
41. honorarium
40. latkes

THE WORDS YOU CONFUSE

46. Just a p - - - - - - - - o?   *a minor fault or offense*
    But it grates like brillo!

47. Her chatter so incessantly i - - - e   *(a) foolish*
    Drove me very nearly insane.
    And gosh, how I'd love to erase
    The oh so s - - - - - - - ious look   *(b) haughty*
    That seems etched into her face.

48. As the candidate (a) _____ for first place
    He (b) _____ aside all who opposed his race.
                                    jockeyed or jostled?

49. When he crashed into her car
    At the j - - - - - - n,   *(a) intersection*
    She was filled with rage;
    He, compunction.
    The accident occurred
    At a j - - - - - - e in his life   *(b) turning point*
    When he seemed bedeviled
    By stress and by strife.

50. Uncle Bud, Aunt Millie, and Cousin Win
    Are my very favorite kissin' k - n.   *(a) relatives*
    My neighbor Marvin and my friend Betty Smith—
    You might say they're my kissin' k - - h.   *(b) friends or*
                                                    relatives.

---

50. (a) kin, (b) kith
49. (a) junction, (b) juncture
48. (a) jockeyed, (b) jostled
47. (a) inane, (b) supercilious
46. peccadillo

117

51. (a) _____ butters your ego,
    Not your bread.
    It's (b) _____ you need
    To stay out of the red.   *lucre or kudos?*

52. My arms feel like cooked spaghetti
    I'm as _____ as yesterday's confetti.
                                         languid or limpid?

53. For a statement untrue
    You may land in a stew.
    Be it l - - - l   *(a) damaging published statements*
    or s - - - - - r,   *(b) damaging things said about someone*
    It'll get up
    Someone's dander.

54. If you are (a) _____
    To crack under duress
    Then being a spy is not (b) _____
    Your best road to success.   *liable or likely?*

55. With our financial situation so impecunious
    Our spirits tend to be rather _____.
                                    salubrious or lugubrious?

---

55. lugubrious
54. (a) liable, (b) likely
53. (a) libel, (b) slander
52. languid
51. (a) kudos, (b) lucre

118

56. His (a) _____ violin playing she adored
But his (b) _____ manner she abhorred.
When the virtuoso's bossiness got worse and worse
She told him to find somewhere else to rehearse.

masterly or masterful?

57. Whether your m - - - - - - e   *(a) lower jaw bone*
or your m - - - - - a takes a hit   *(b) upper jaw bone*
It'll hurt more than a little bit.

58. (a) _____s are rhetorical tools to compare
Two dissimilar ideas with color and flare.
Flag the comparison with *as if*, *like* or *as*
And add the element of surprise for snap and pizazz.

The (b) _____ is the (a) _____ 's kin
But with an implicit and more subtle spin.
Instead of comparing one thing to another
Figuratively speaking, it becomes the other.

metaphor or simile?

59. A tiny rodent whose tail goes swish
Fast asleep in your best dish?
Plus a look-alike critter twice the size,
What on earth *is* this double surprise?

ANSWER: The guy in your dish is a harmless mouse
But, yikes, you've also got a rat in your house.

---

58. (a) similes, (b) metaphor, (a) simile
57. (a) mandible, (b) maxilla
56. (a) masterly, (b) masterful

60. Her pizazz made her more n - - - - - - - - e *(a) easily noticed*
    Than the celebrated visiting n - - - - - e. *(b) someone*
    renowned

61. If by a nickname or pseudonym you're known
    It's not the one given you when you were born.
    NICKNAME: *(a) alias, (b) informal or stage name*
    PSEUDONYM: *(a) stage or pen name, (b) alias*

62. Our o - - - - - ious host, Mr. Daugherty *overly obliging*
    Treated us just like visiting royalty.

63. A/An (a) _____ aged seventy plus five . . .
    That's my grandma, brimming with life.
    A/An (b) _____ of eighty plus nine . . .
    That's grandpa, who's also doing fine.
    septuagenarian or octogenarian?

64. It's o - - - - - - - l, *(a) a formal fact*
    I assure you all
    that o - - - - - - - - s lout *(b) bossy, imperious*
    Is in for a fall!

---

64. (a) official, (b) officious
63. (a) septuagenarian, (b) octogenarian
62. obsequious
61. nickname (b), pseudonym (a)
60. (a) noticeable, (b) notable

120

65. If wordplay is
    Your kind of
    Enjoyment,
    Why not with
    Palindromes,
    Pleonasms or
    Oxymorons
    Experiment?
    (Pick one answer for each:)
         PALINDROME: *(a) the same spelling forward or backward*
                    (b) spelled-alike words with different meanings.
         PLEONASM: *(a) redundant words, (b) contradictory words*
         OXYMORON: *(a) redundant words, (b) contradictory words*

66. QUESTION: How can I make my parrot petite?

    ANSWER: Trade it in for a parakeet.

67. Family traditions are worth (a) _____
    But a crime is not what you want to be (b) _____.
                              perpetrating or perpetuating?

68. One who's p - - - - - - - - ious   *(a) very perceptive*
    Is shrewd and sagacious
    A speaker who's p - - - - - - - ous   *(b) clear, understandable*
    Will never ever confuse us.

---

68. (a) perspicacious, (b) perspicuous
67. (a) perpetuating, (b) perpetrating
65. palindrome (a), pleonasm (a), oxymoron (b)

121

69. A single cat that weighs a ton.
    Is a rare p - - - - - - - n.   *(a) single rarity*
    Many cats singing opera?
    They'd be rare-as-rare p - - - - - - - a.   *(b) multiple rarities*

70. Because the descent involved
    Some (a) _____ drops
    The climbers neither yodeled
    Or took (b) _____ hops.

    precipitate or precipitous?

71. For neighborhood peace I would p - - - - - -   *(a) advise*
    That horn tooting after midnight you p - - - - - - - e.

    (b) forbid

72. I brought home a pretty puss
    Who was sweet but p - - - - - - - - - ous   *(a) cowardly*
    Today she's fat and quite ungracious
    And if you cross her, quite p - - - - - ious   *(b) combative*

73. QUESTION: If a poodle's forebears are poodles all
    Into what category would that poodle fall?
    And if you marry a schnauzer to a poodle
    What breed then would claim their schnoodle?

    ANSWER: The poodle's a pure breed,
    The schnoodle a cross breed.

---

72. (a) pusillanimous, (b) pugnacious
71. (a) prescribe, (b) proscribe
70. (a) precipitous, (b) precipitate
69. (a) phenomenon, (b) phenomena

74. I hate
    like hell
    Their fun
    to _____.   *quell or quench?*

75. Her bursts of rhetoric s - - - - - - c   *(a) occasional*
    Are full of notions quite q - - - - - - c.   *(b) impractical*

76. I feel more r - - - - - e   *(a) uneasy*
    than r - - - - - l or festive.   *(b) relaxed*

77. Frankly, my dear, I'm r - - - - - - t   *(a) disinclined*
    to spend my life with Millicent.
    My reason you ask? Well I simply can't
    Live with someone as t - - - - - - n as a plant.
                                                    (b) uncommunicative

78. We exposed his _____
    So he went on the lam.   *scam or sham?*

79. The song was a number one hit
    Thanks to its _____ wit.

                                    scintillating or titillating?

---

79. scintillating
78. scam
77. (a) reticent (b) taciturn
76. (a) restive, (b) restful
75. (a) sporadic, (b) quixotic
74. quell

123

80. Trouble that can't be undone, I s - - n.   *(a) avoid*
    A bargain I cannot return, I s - - - n.   *(b) reject, disdain*

81. QUESTION: Why build a church with a steeple but not a
    spire?

ANSWER: If a tower without a point you admire.

82. Just as one cup of flour
    Will not bake a cake
    So a single line of v - - - e   *(a) line of poetry*
    Does not a s - - - - a make.   *(b) lines forming poetic section*

83. When a pronoun introduces information that's a must
    And without it the sentence would be a meaningless bust
    (a) _____ is correct to select.

    But what if the sentence remains solid
    Even if the clause is removed from it?
    Then (b) _____ is correct to select.   *that or which?*

84. As they travelled the long, hot and (a) _____ path
    They found it (b) _____ not to have water for a bath.
                                   tortuous or torturous?

---

84. (a) tortuous, (b) torturous
83. (a) that, (b) which
82. (a) verse, (b) stanza
80. (a) shun, (b) spurn

124

85. Prose (a) _____ with words from antiquity
    Is too (b) _____ to communicate with clarity.
    turgid or turbid?

86. When a friend doesn't give you a birthday gift
    It's a v - - - - l social sin and not worth a rift.   *venal or*
    venial?

87. The (a) _____ looks like a (b) _____ clone
    But it's bigger and gives a mellower tone.
    violin or viola?

88. If you _____ me as a man immoral
    Be prepared for a rousing quarrel.   *vilify or vivify?*

89. As more power for himself he _____
    In a web of deceit he became entangled.
    wangled or wrangled?

90. Whenever (a) _____ across (b) _____ is passed
    You get a fabric made to last.
    This meaning extends to any structure
    Strong enough to resist rupture.
    Some say the United States Constitution
    Is our warp and weft as an institution.
    warp or weft?

---

90. (a) weft, (b) warp
89. wangled
88. vilify
87. (a) viola, (b) violin
86. venial
85. (a) turgid, (b) turbid

125

91. You're too w - - y, my dear heart   *(a) cunning*
    So I think that we should part.
    You see, I'm w - - y of pursuing   *(b) cautious*
    An affair I may start ruing.

92. Things that on a w - - m you do   *(a) without rational*
    You will often bitterly rue.   *thought*
    Ideas that overflow with w - - - - y *(b) fanciful ideas*
    May turn out to be too flimsy

93. If you want to feel fully alive,
    For a balance between y - n and y - - g
    You should strive.

                    (a) passivity, darkness
                    (b) assertiveness, light

---

93. (a) yin, (b) yang
92. (a) whim, (b) whimsy
91. (a) wily, (b) wary

Index of Words

Throughout the text entries are alphabetically arranged according to the first word defined. Here every word from the text is alphabetized. Words in parentheses refer you to the first word of the entry where you will find the definition.

A

abdicate, 3
abridgement, 3
abrogate (abdicate), 3
abyss, 3
ac, 3
acclimation, 3
acculturation (acclimation), 3
accusation, 4
acme, 4
acquiescent, 4
acronym, 4
across-the-board, 4
acute, 5
ad hoc, 5
ad lib (ad hoc), 5
adapt, 5

C

D

E

G

H

K

L

margarine (butter), 23
market value (book value), 21
marsh, 73
marsupial (mammal), 73
masochist, 73
mass-market paperback, 73
mastectomy (lumpectomy), 71
masterful, 74
masterly (masterful), 74
maxilla (mandible), 73
meadow (field), 55
measles (German measles), 59
meat loaf, 74
mediator (arbitrator), 14
melody, 74
mendacious, 74
mercurial, 74
meretricious, 75
meritorious (meretricious), 75
metaphor, 75
meteor (asteroid), 15
meteoroid (asteroid), 15
meteorite (asteroid), 15
meticulous, 75
mezzo-soprano (alto), 8
migrant (emigrant), 48
mildew, 75
milestone (capstone), 26
militate, 75
Minotaur (centaur), 27
misanthrope, 76
misdemeanor (felony), 54
mishap (contretemps), 34
misogamist (misanthrope), 76
misogynist (misanthrope), 76
mist (fog), 56
mitigate (militate), 75

Modified American Plan (American Plan), 9
modus operandi, 76
modus vivendi (modus operandi), 76
mold (mildew), 75
momentous, 76
monotheistic, 76
monumental (momentous), 76
moth (butterfly), 23
mouse, 76
mousse, 76
multiple (manifold), 73
munificent (magnificent), 72
munitions (ammunition), 10
musical, 76
mutt (crossbreed), 37
myth (legend), 70

nadir, 77
nauseate, 77
nauseous (nauseate), 77
nautical mile, 77
nectar (ambrosia), 9
nefarious, 77
negligent (desultory), 40
negligible (desultory), 41
net earnings (gross earnings), 61
neurotic, 77
nickname, 77
nocturnal (diurnal), 44
noisome (fulsome), 58
nondifferentiated cancer (differentiated cancer), 42

notable, 78
noticeable (notable), 78
notorious (nefarious), 77
novice (amateur), 9
number (amount), 10
numismatist, 78
nymphomaniac, 78

O

obese (corpulent), 36
obfuscation, 78
Obie (Emmy), 58
obscene, 78
obsequious, 79
obstreperous (boisterous), 21
obtuseness (obfuscation), 79
octogenarian, 79
octopus, 79
off-Broadway, 79
off-off Broadway (off-Broadway), 79
official, 79
officious (official), 79
ohms (amps), 10
on the contrary, 79
on the nose (across-the-board), 4
oncology, 80
one another (each other), 45
ontology (oncology), 80
opera, 80
ophthalmologist, 80
opposite (apposite), 13
opprobrium (encomium), 48

prognosis (diagnosis), 41
proofreader (copy editor), 35
prophesy (presage), 86
propriety (probity), 86
proscribe (prescribe), 86
prosody, 87
prostate, 87
prostrate (prostate), 87
prototype (paradigm), 82
prudent, 87
pseudonym (nickname), 78
psychiatrist, 87
psychologist, clinical (psychiatrist), 88
psychotherapist (psychiatrist), 88
psychotic (neurotic), 77
public domain (fair use), 53
pugnacious, 88
pungent (cogent), 30
pure breed (crossbreed), 37
purvey, 88
purview (purvey), 88
pusillanimous (pugnacious), 88

Q

quagmire, 88
quake, 88
qualitative, 88
quantitative (qualitative), 88
quarrelsome, 89
queasy, 89
quell, 89
quench (quell), 89

querulous (quarrelsome), 89
quicksand (quagmire), 88
quiescent (acquiescent), 4
quintessential (penultimate), 83
quiver (quake), 88
quixotic, 89
quorum, 89
quota (quorum), 89

R

radiotherapy (chemotherapy), 28
radius (circumference), 29
rain forest (jungle), 68
RAM (CD-ROM), 27
ram (ewe), 51
ramble, 89
random access memory (CD-ROM), 27
range (ramble), 89
rap (pop), 85
rare, 90
rat (mouse), 76
ratify, 90
read only memory (CD-ROM), 27
rebuff, 90
rebut (rebuff), 90
recital (concert), 32
recrimination (accusation), 4
redolent, 90
reduced fat (low fat), 70
redundant (redolent), 90
referee, 90
referendum (plebiscite), 85

S

T

W

X

Y

Z

About the Author

ELYSE SOMMER has compiled two collections of similes (. . . *As One Mad with Wine* and *Falser than a Weeping Crocodile*), a children's thesaurus of colorful phrase (*I Read You Loud and Clear*), and a children's music almanac (*The Kids' World Almanac of Music*). She is also an author's representative.